IMPROVING SCHOOLS

IMPROVING SCHOOLS
Performance and Potential

**John Gray, David Hopkins, David Reynolds,
Brian Wilcox, Shaun Farrell, David Jesson**

OPEN UNIVERSITY PRESS
Buckingham · Philadelphia

Open University Press
Celtic Court
22 Ballmoor
Buckingham
MK18 1XW

email: enquiries@openup.co.uk
world wide web: http://www.openup.co.uk

and

325 Chestnut Street
Philadelphia, PA 19106, USA

First Published 1999

A catalogue record of this book is available from the British Library

ISBN   0 335 20399 X (hb) 0 335 20398 1 (pb)

Library of Congress Cataloging-in-Publication Data
Improving schools: performance and potential / John Gray . . . [et al.].
    p. cm.
    Includes bibliographical references (p.) and indexes.
    ISBN 0–335–20399–X (hb). – ISBN 0–335–20398–1 (pb)
    1. School improvement programs–Great Britain–Case studies.
2. Academic achievement–Great Britain–Case studies. 3. School
management and organization–Great Britain–Case studies.
4. Educational change–Great Britain–Case studies. I. Gray. John
(John Michael), 1948–
LB2822.84.G7T68 1999
371.2′00941–dc21   98–45148
                                                              CIP

Typeset by Graphicraft Ltd, Hong Kong
Printed in Great Britain by Biddles Ltd, Guildford and King's Lynn

CONTENTS

ACKNOWLEDGEMENTS

The members of the Improving Schools Research Project would like to record their sincere thanks to the 12 schools which agreed to allow themselves to be studied in some depth. Unfortunately, promises about confidentiality prohibit us from naming them here.

The research has been supported by a grant from the Economic and Social Research Council (R000235864) to John Gray, David Hopkins and David Reynolds. We would like to record our thanks to the ESRC for its support, but the views and opinions expressed here remain, of course, our own responsibility. We are also most grateful to the officers of the three LEAs in which we have been working for the support they have given us in gaining access to their schools and for ironing out minor problems as the research has proceeded. We would also like to thank the Analytical Services Branch of the Department for Education and Employment who kindly provided the data on which some of the national analyses are based as well as the disks from which the national database on schools was constructed.

Harvey Goldstein acted as statistical consultant during the initial phase of the project for the multi-level modelling aspect of the analyses in relation to our first LEA. Julia Wilcox and Avril Silk helped with some of the school interviews as well as the coding and transcription of the data, while Alan Russell was responsible for preparing the manuscript.

LIST OF FIGURES AND TABLES

THE RISE OF SCHOOL IMPROVEMENT

The growth of interest in 'school improvement' has been striking. In less than a decade the educational system has moved from a position where changes in performance from one year to the next were so small as barely to excite comment to one where 'improvement' has not merely been expected but demanded. Schools now have to set 'improvement' targets and local education authorities have to demonstrate how they have been 'contributing to school improvement' (Office for Standards in Education (Ofsted) 1997b). How actively schools will embrace the notion of 'continuous improvement', however, remains to be seen.

It is tempting to imagine that the school system has been undergoing something of a cultural transformation in recent years. The conflicting debris from long-standing debates about standards in education, however, counsels a degree of caution. Comparisons of standards over time, on a like-with-like basis, are notoriously difficult to undertake (see Goldstein and Lewis 1996; Newton 1997). Furthermore, as both historians and analysts of school reform remind us, educational systems are typically both slow to change and prone to resist reform (Silver 1994; Fullan 1993). None the less, and in the shorter term, there are *some* promising signs, not least because the need for schools to improve is now more widely recognized.

The most obvious evidence for the 'rise of school improvement' in England and Wales can be noted in the upward trend of the 'headline' statistics in recent years (Gray and Jesson 1996). Before 1988 the proportion of pupils obtaining more than five A–C passes at O-level barely changed from year to year. Indeed, if it had fluctuated by more than a small amount some form of public inquiry would doubtless have been called for. Between 1988 and 1996, however, the figure rose at an historically unprecedented rate. Policy-makers did not merely note the rises

– many welcomed them and excoriated detractors. The seeds of heightened expectations were clearly being planted.

The year 1988, of course, witnessed the introduction of the General Certificate of Secondary Education (GCSE) examination, with its promise of a grade (of some sort) for virtually all those who entered. The same year also saw the introduction of the National Curriculum, with its core diet of subjects. In combination, these two factors began to fuel improvement. First, if virtually all grades of entry were awarded some sort of pass then it made little sense to withdraw pupils (as had been the previous custom) for fear they might not do well. And second, if all pupils were obliged to study particular subjects (as part of the National Curriculum) for the greater part of their secondary school careers, then it made equally little sense to withdraw them from the exams during their final months of preparation. In the four years after their introduction most schools began to take advantage of these various changes – the idea that schools might improve had begun to take root.

So-called 'league tables' of secondary schools' exam results were first published in the national press in late 1992. Again, just as in the earlier period, there was a common response from the vast majority of schools – the average number of exams for which pupils were entered rose by around one entry per pupil within the space of a year. This appears to have been a one-off response. Subsequently, schools acted in a wide variety of other ways as well launching, in the process, numerous 'school improvement' initiatives. The idea that schools might improve their performance from year to year began to take root. However, while many of these initiatives were undoubtedly quite ambitious, their combined effects, measured at least in terms of pupil outcomes, appear to have been more modest. Year-on-year increases during the period 1988–92 ran at approximately double those occurring during 1992–96.

The need to merge research traditions

When we began our research we believed we were building on fairly solid foundations. After all, there were more than two decades of work on school effectiveness to draw upon and at least a decade's work explicitly focused on school improvement (Reynolds *et al.* 1996). The task, as we initially saw it, was to shift the focus away from what makes a school effective at any particular point in time towards a greater understanding of how schools become more effective over time. On closer examination, however, we discovered that the knowledge base was less firmly founded and rather more lop-sided than we had originally anticipated.

On the school effectiveness side there was a very considerable body of evidence on the nature and patterning of school effects. Estimates of their extent and range were well established with contributions from around the world. Given their ready availability, most of this work has concentrated on exam and test results although the need for broader and alternative perspectives is sometimes acknowledged. Many of the correlates of school effectiveness have also been extensively explored through a mixture of quantitatively- and qualitatively-oriented studies – see Sammons *et al.* (1997) for an up-to-date review and Hopkins *et al.* (1994), Myers (1996) and National Commission on Education (1996) for some evidence on individual schools. After more than two decades of research it seems fair to claim that quite a lot was known about the nature of so-called 'effective' schools, although the precise status of the knowledge base has remained a matter for debate – see Barber and White (1997) for some contemporary critiques.

There was a similarly large body of evidence on the nature of school improvement; see Stoll and Fink (1996) and Hargreaves *et al.* (1998) for extensive reviews. Again researchers of both quantitative and qualitative persuasions have made contributions, although the latter have been rather more dominant. On closer examination, however, we found that most of the research to date has been about the *processes* of school improvement; very little has focused on the outcomes, or the links between processes and outcomes, which have simply been assumed or ignored. There is a danger, however, in making sweeping generalizations about differences between the two approaches. Researchers of both persuasions seem very interested indeed in both pupil outcomes and school processes – the main barrier has been the lack of evidence (Reynolds *et al.* 1993).

So, given that there is a degree of overlap in terms of the key questions, why has it proved so difficult to merge the two traditions? Much of the answer, we believe, boils down to the old adage that the data researchers have available (or think they could obtain without disproportionate effort) tend to structure the questions that get asked and the questions that get asked tend to structure the data that are collected (along with views about what additional evidence could reasonably be collected). The fact that school improvement usually takes place over lengthy periods of time is unfortunate but inescapable. How researchers have chosen to handle the time dimension, therefore, has crucially affected the nature of the research they have undertaken and the interpretations of the resulting evidence they have offered. A typical school effectiveness study, for example, has usually been confined to a cross-sectional survey at one point in time or a longitudinal study of the experiences of a single cohort of students. On those rare occasions when data on a second cohort have been collected they have usually been employed to confirm the findings from analyses of the first cohort. The driving concern has been with the stability of school effects over time. As we have observed elsewhere, some degree of instability is needed for changes in schools' performance to be observed (Gray and Wilcox 1995). Regrettably, the baggage of assumptions which researchers have brought to their analyses has simply ruled this out.

Studies of school improvement have been similarly circumscribed. Researchers within this tradition have undoubtedly been interested in the effects of processes on pupil performance but the time-scales to which they too have adhered and their beliefs about how long worthwhile innovations take to become established have almost invariably made data collection difficult.

Several other problems have been identified in the literature. The focus on effectiveness has been a static one. It has been difficult to study how schools have become more effective over time in the absence of routinely collected data on pupil outcomes. Furthermore, in both effectiveness and improvement studies, the 'site' of the 'ineffective' school has not been systematically studied due to 'sampling difficulties' (an obvious euphemism). There has also been a tendency to adopt an undifferentiated perspective in relation to the identification of appropriate strategies for change; too little attention has been given to what has come to be known as 'context-specificity' (Teddlie and Stringfield 1993).

In recent years the need to bring the two approaches closer together and to create a merged paradigm has begun to be accepted; see various contributions from leading researchers to Gray et al. (1996b) and MacBeath and Mortimore (1994). This emerging paradigm is more concerned to relate the processes of school improvement to outcomes than previously and recognizes the need to study the full variety of changes going on within schools – including changes at the classroom level. Given the extent to which schools tend to initiate changes simultaneously on several fronts, the paradigm is more sceptical about single-cause explanations of improvement and recognizes some of the advantages of mixing methods to study them. Finally, it is more aware of 'context-specificity' and consequently more cautious about how far findings can be transferred from one context to another.

Towards a definition of school improvement

When we reflected on the definitions of 'improvement' which had been used in previous research we found most of them lacking (Gray 1997); indeed often the meaning they attributed to 'improvement' was left implicit. As the historian Harold Silver might have observed: ' "Improving" has been an infinitely adaptable epithet, used of schools and initiatives of many kinds, used by interested parties of many kinds . . . an improving school has usually been one which satisfies the subjective sentiments of its controllers, participants or clients'.[1]

The definition of 'improvement' we decided to adopt was framed within the traditions of earlier research on school effectiveness (see Gray and

Wilcox 1995) but also reflected concerns which had been raised in the improvement research (Hopkins *et al.* 1994). An 'improving' school in our study was one which 'increased in its effectiveness' over time. In other words, the amounts of 'value-added' it generated for its pupils would be expected to rise for successive cohorts. While we believe our definition will eventually come to be seen as the most satisfactory approach to this issue, it has to be recognized that no previous study, to the best of our knowledge, has defined improvement in comparable terms. This definition is likely to have implications for what kinds of activities might count as 'school improvement'. It gives particular salience to efforts towards change which focus on student achievement and the classroom and organizational conditions which support it.

One obvious reason for this omission is that insufficient data have been available. To establish a reasonably robust estimate of a secondary school's effectiveness at a single point in time (its 'value-added'), information on pupils' progress (say from the age of 11 to the age of 16) is required. It follows that to establish whether a school has *changed* in its effectiveness further estimates from comparable cohorts in subsequent years are needed. Indeed, in order to begin to discern whether there are trends in effectiveness over time a minimum of three such estimates is essential – and more are desirable. An 'improving' school, therefore, may be defined as one which 'increases in its effectiveness' over time, where 'effectiveness' is judged in value-added terms.

The strategy we developed for describing schools located them in two dimensions: in terms of their initial effectiveness and their subsequent improvement trajectories. We knew a good deal from previous studies about how differences between schools in their effectiveness were distributed and felt reasonably confident in placing schools in one of three groups: those which were clearly of 'above average' effectiveness, given their intakes; those which were of 'average' effectiveness; and those which were clearly of 'below average' effectiveness. We also knew from previous work that roughly two-thirds to three-quarters of all schools would fall into the 'average' category while the remaining one-quarter to one-third would be fairly evenly distributed between the other two categories.

Our understanding of the improvement dimension was more tentative. We guessed, on the basis of previous knowledge about the relative stability of school effects over two years, that the greater proportion of the variation in pupils' performance potentially attributable to schools was probably captured by the 'effectiveness' dimension.[2] However, we could not be sure of this. We simply lacked information about whether what held across two consecutive cohorts applied equally strongly when performance was reviewed across four or five. Furthermore, we had little or no knowledge of whether schools 'improved' (or 'deteriorated') in their effectiveness in more consistent ways over a number of years. Were there signs, in other words, that some schools had found ways of locking into continuous improvement trajectories, or was progress through short bursts more common? And finally, what were schools' rates of improvement? Given that a school was consistently improving from year to year, how quickly could it move from one 'level' of effectiveness to another? The answer to this particular question depends on knowing not merely the distances between groups of schools of comparable effectiveness but also something about the rates at which schools can move to eliminate them.

Towards a research strategy

There were several starting-points, therefore, for the current study, which was funded over a period of two years by the Economic and Social Research Council (ESRC). The first was the increasing recognition of the need to combine the techniques, approaches and perspectives of the 'school effectiveness' and 'school improvement' traditions. A second was the realization that, to date, we have lacked a study conducted within an initially quantitative framework, either in the United Kingdom or elsewhere, of the extent of 'naturally occurring' school improvement and the factors contributing to it. And the third was the existence of some data-sets which could help us to start asking what we had come to see as the most appropriate questions.

Consequently, we set about seeking answers to three key concerns. First, we wanted to develop better estimates of the extent to which schools had changed in their effectiveness over time. With a stronger framework than previous researchers for judging improvement, we hoped to be in a better position to address our second concern, which was to try to understand more about some of the factors and strategies associated with changes in performance across schools. Such a framework could also help us with our third concern, to get close up to the school improvement process in order to learn more about the difficulties and challenges to be faced on the route to improvement. For this purpose a series of case studies of schools – in particular, 'ineffective' schools – seemed most appropriate.

Notes

1 Adapted with apologies from Silver's comments on the use of the term 'good' in relation to schools (see Silver 1994: 6).
2 The correlations relating to schools' effectiveness across two consecutive cohorts of pupils have been uniformly high; see Chapter 11 of Gray and Wilcox (1995) for a fuller account of the relevant research.

▶ ▶ ▷ **Part I**

FRAMEWORKS AND ASSUMPTIONS

A NATION ON THE MOVE?

One fact seems incontrovertible – in recent years performance levels, judged in terms of exam passes at 16+, have been rising. We certainly seem to be a nation on the move. What has triggered these changes? To what extent have we been reaping the rewards of earlier system-wide initiatives? And how far have these been matched (or driven) by developments at the level of the individual school? In short, has the school improvement 'dividend' now been largely secured or is there potentially more to come?

Pupils' performance in public examinations has, in fact, been rising since the mid-1970s – at times rather slowly, sometimes more rapidly. Figure 2.1 covers the two decades during which public examinations have not only moved on to a common basis (the GCSE) but also increasingly become a suitable target for all young people. It shows the position for four separate indicators. The third of these has, historically at least, been viewed as a relatively 'high' hurdle. In 1975, just under a quarter of the age cohort obtained five or more A–C grades (or their equivalents); by 1995 this had risen to well over 40 per cent. During these two decades the proportions of the age cohort *presented* for public examination also rose.

The publication of annual performance tables focused interest on these 'headline statistics' (especially the proportions of the age cohort securing five or more A–C grades). Table 2.1 considers the year-on-year changes over the last two decades. This particular table shows the increases using the previous year's figures as the base. It is evident that from 1975 to 1987 the changes were generally very modest. There was a slight increase in the mid to late seventies, following the raising of the school leaving age, and again in the early 1980s. But overall the rate of change was very marginal indeed.[1]

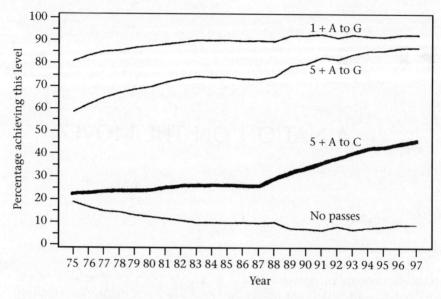

Figure 2.1 Examination results at 16+ from 1974–75 to 1996–97

Table 2.1 Year-on-year increases in age cohort obtaining five or more A–C passes

1976 (on 1975)	1%	1987 (on 1986)	−1%
1977	3%	1988	13%
1978	1%	1989	10%
1979	0%	1990	5%
1980	1%	1991	7%
1981	4%	1992	4%
1982	4%	1993	8%
1983	0%	1994	5%
1984	2%	1995	0%
1985	1%	1996	2%
1986	−1%	1997	1%

The introduction of the GCSE in 1988 (a common examination for all which replaced the earlier system of O levels for a minority and CSEs for the majority) seems to have heralded an era of more substantial year-on-year changes. By the standards of the earlier ones outlined above, all the increases from 1988 to 1997 were sizeable. Again, however, this period can be subdivided. The rate of increase between 1988 and 1992 appears to have been approximately double that between 1992 and 1997. This is of interest in so far as the latter period is the time when publication of the performance tables is assumed to have stimulated schools' interest in improving their exam results. However, it is the period when schools were learning how to respond to the opportunities afforded by the GCSE which appears to have brought the greater year-on-year gains.

Changes at the level of the school

We were also interested in changes at the level of the individual school. To explore this we had to construct an overall data-set on schools' performances from the annual league tables published in 1992, 1993, 1994 and 1995 (Gray and Jesson 1996). This had the advantage that it was reasonably comprehensive in terms of national coverage (over 3000 schools were represented) but suffered from two major drawbacks: a lack of information about differences between schools in terms of intakes; and the consequent difficulty of undertaking anything but the most elementary of statistical analyses.

Figure 2.1 shows that between 1992 and 1995 the proportion of the age cohort achieving five or more A*–C passes rose from around 38 per cent to 43 per cent. To keep pace with national developments a typical school would, therefore, have had to achieve a five percentage-point increase in the number of its pupils achieving this level of performance. The majority of schools clearly did so.[2] However, Figure 2.2, which compares each school's performance in 1992 with its subsequent performance in 1995, suggests that many schools managed to 'improve' by a good deal more than this. A school located on the slanting diagonal performed at the same level in 1995 as in 1992; schools which are above the line did 'better' in 1995 than in 1992. Even a cursory glance indicates that very large numbers managed to raise their performance.

To what extent did schools from different starting bands make comparable amounts of progress? We divided the schools in the database into seven broad groups (see Table 2.2), according to their starting levels of performance in 1992, and then calculated the average improvement for each group. It is evident from the table that schools in the lowest group (those with 0–10 per cent of their pupils obtaining five or more A*–C passes in 1992) averaged just over a 5 per cent increase by 1995. The increases for four of the other groups (the 11–20, 21–30, 31–40 and 41–50 per cent bands) were very similar. For the two highest starting bands (51–60 and 61–100 per cent) the increases were about a percentage point lower.[3] Table 2.2 also suggests that schools were not able, on average, to maintain the same increases over each of the separate years. In most cases the increases were largest between 1992 and 1993 and, in every case, the increases between 1994 and 1995 were more modest than those in the earlier period.

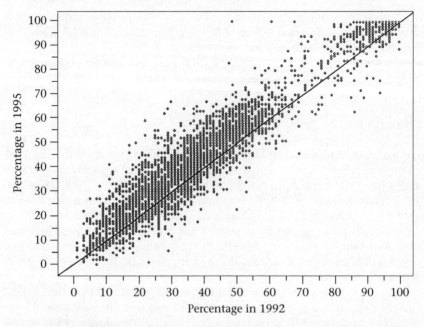

Figure 2.2 Change and improvement in schools achieving five or more A*–C passes, 1992–95

Table 2.2 Average increases in percentages obtaining five or more A*–C passes, broken down by school's starting band in 1992

School's starting band in 1992	Average increase for schools in band			
	1992–95	*1992–93*	*1993–94*	*1994–95*
0–10%	5.3	3.7	1.4	0.2
11–20%	5.5	3.2	1.9	0.4
21–30%	5.5	3.1	1.5	0.9
31–40%	4.9	2.4	2.4	0.1
41–50%	5.4	2.1	2.7	0.6
51–60%	3.8	0.5	2.1	1.2
61–100%	3.4	1.2	1.8	0.4

The cumulative effects of these increases on the distribution of schools across the starting bands can be seen in Table 2.3. Whereas about one in five schools had 20 per cent or less of their pupils obtaining five or more A*–C passes in 1992, this proportion fell to about one in eight in 1995.

Table 2.3 Percentages of schools in each of the starting bands between 1992 and 1995

Starting band	Percentage of all schools in band			
	1992	1993	1994	1995
0–10%	5.5	4.1	3.5	2.7
11–20%	14.6	12.9	10.9	10.0
21–30%	19.2	18.1	16.6	15.8
31–40%	20.7	19.1	18.6	17.9
41–50%	16.7	18.2	18.5	18.4
51–60%	9.2	12.3	14.0	15.1
61–100%	14.1	15.4	17.9	20.1
	(100.0)	(100.0)	(100.0)	(100.0)

The effects in the lowest band were more dramatic. Initially one of the 'triggers' employed by Ofsted's inspectors to judge whether a school was at risk of 'failing' was whether it fell into this band. In 1992, just over 5 per cent of schools performed at this level; by 1995 this figure had been halved.

Patterns of change in individual schools

It is obvious from the evidence we have already presented that the greater majority of schools managed to secure some increases in the performances of their pupils between 1992 and 1995. But, equally obviously, some schools increased more rapidly than others. How did these gains occur? Did they happen in a single year or did some schools manage to sustain increases over each of the three years in turn? Increases concentrated in a single year might suggest that a school was simply 'catching up' or beginning to 'get back on track'. More sustained year-on-year changes, on the other hand, might indicate that a school had developed a more systematic approach to school improvement.

Table 2.4 indicates that around one school in seven fell into our 'improving' schools category. The proportions of schools in each starting band, however, varied. For the five lower starting bands the proportion was around 15 per cent. For the two highest starting bands these figures were rather lower at under ten per cent. In the case of the 61–100 per cent band it should, of course, be remembered that some schools were already too close to the 'ceiling' to achieve increases of this order.

Table 2.4   Percentages of 'improving' schools, broken down by school's starting band in 1992

Starting band	Percentage of 'improving' schools*
0–10%	15%
11–20%	16%
21–30%	18%
31–40%	15%
41–50%	15%
51–60%	9%
61–100%	8%

* To meet the criteria for inclusion as an 'improving' school, an institution had to have improved its 1995 results by *at least* the average improvement for all schools over the period from 1992 (4.9%) plus one standard deviation (7.7%), making a total of 12.6%.

Table 2.5   Nature of improvement secured by 'improving' schools, broken down by school's starting band in 1992 (%)

Starting band*	'Consistent'**	'Uneven'	'Volatile'	Total
0–10%	67	17	17	101
11–20%	66	17	17	100
21–30%	62	19	19	100
31–40%	68	19	13	100
41–50%	66	16	18	100

* The table is confined to the 5 lower starting bands where the proportion of 'improving' schools was 15% or more (see Table 2.4).
** A school was defined as a 'consistent' improver if its year-on-year increases from 1992 to 1995 were monotonic, as an 'uneven' improver if the increases monotonically were ±3%, and as 'volatile' if there was considerable inter-year variation.

The patterns of year-on-year change for the one in seven schools which fell into the 'improving school' category are described in Table 2.5. Overall, we concluded that about two-thirds of the 'improving schools' had achieved their year-on-year increases in a 'consistent' fashion; the proportions were very similar across the starting bands. The remaining third were divided equally between what we termed 'uneven' and 'volatile' groups. The 'uneven' group might have made rather greater progress in one year than the next, but the year-on-year pattern was generally upwards. The 'volatile' group was made up from the remainder which failed to meet the criteria for inclusion in the first two groups. Some schools in this group achieved all their improvements in a single year, with static or even declining results for the other two.

This analysis is of interest because it suggests that around two-thirds of schools were improving in ways that were sufficiently 'consistent' to justify the hypothesis that there was something substantial and enduring behind their change processes. It does not, of course, guarantee it; more sophisticated procedures, which take account of differences in schools' intakes, are required. What the analysis does show, however, is that only about one in ten schools nationally appear to have been improving 'consistently'.[4]

The greater majority of schools produced results in 1995, at least in relation to the five or more A*–C passes hurdle, which were above those they had secured in 1992. They could, therefore, be said in some sense to have been 'improving'. However, we should perhaps reiterate that between the same two points in time the national proportion getting over this hurdle rose from 38 per cent to 43 per cent making a five percentage-point increase in performance, necessary to keep pace with national trends. A school which made less progress than this might well appear, at first sight, to have improved its performance since 1992; however, in relative terms it would actually have fallen behind. An unexpected feature thrown up by this analysis was that, almost across the board, schools made their largest gains in the first year (that is between 1992 and 1993); in subsequent years the increases in performance became progressively smaller.

For a school to be seen to be pulling ahead of the pack, considerably greater increases than those outlined above would be required. We estimated that about one in seven schools were clearly doing so. However, within this group of schools, only two-thirds could be said to be improving 'consistently' from year to year. In the remaining third of cases we characterised the schools' improvement trajectories as 'uneven' or even 'volatile'. They might manage a sizeable step one year and then fall back a bit the next.

In sum, while most secondary schools can point to some improvement in performance over the past few years, at least when judged by 'raw' results, the greater majority have simply been keeping up with national trends and developments. Schools which appeared to be improving 'rapidly' *and* consistently, ahead of the pack, made up only around one in ten of all schools nationally.

Possible explanations for the changes at national level

A variety of influences have probably contributed to the increases in pupils' performance. Many seem to have operated across the whole system and affected all schools to a greater or lesser extent; others have probably been confined to smaller numbers of schools.

The introduction of the GCSE and the National Curriculum

The introduction of the GCSE in 1988 seems to have triggered the first set of rises in performance. Certainly the transition to the new system in 1988 brought about a very sizeable increase on the position in 1987. But this does not seem to have been simply a 'blip' in the statistics; nearly every year since then the increases have continued to be sizeable when judged by previous standards.

The GCSE reform provided common examination targets for all pupils, with a common grading system in which all levels of performance received some recognition. The increases in pupils' performance which followed in the three or four years after its initial introduction were the largest on record in the last two decades.

The introduction of the National Curriculum, also in 1988, may well have contributed to this changed climate of assumptions, although its effects are unlikely to have occurred all at once and probably unravelled during the early 1990s as well. Schools probably realized that if their pupils had studied a subject up to a time not too distant from the final examinations, then there was some merit in encouraging them to stay the course. Entering a subject is, of course, a precondition for being graded in it and all but the very lowest levels of performance would be rewarded by a grade. Consequently, the risks of presenting pupils 'inappropriately' may have been felt to have been reduced.

Accompanying the introduction of the GCSE and the National Curriculum, there seems to have been a shift in the way in which people judged schools' exam performances. The common exam and the (notionally) common curriculum signalled the importance of a common framework for evaluating outcomes. In the early 1980s the most frequently employed yardstick for judgement was the 'pass rate'. The weakness of this statistic was, of course, that it was dependent on decisions about which pupils should be entered for an exam, and could be easily 'manipulated'. Different schools made different decisions about entering apparently comparable pupils. By the late 1980s national statistics based on the whole cohort of pupils had become the modal approach although not, it should be said, the only one.[5]

The introduction of the GCSE and the National Curriculum heralded more specific changes in the nature of the examinations on offer. The development of 'balanced' or 'combined' science (which counts as two passes) is one example of a more general attempt to ensure that appropriate exam targets were available for all pupils. Alongside such developments some components of the curriculum were 'restructured' as exam options; by Years 10 and 11 the time for non-examined subjects had become, in most schools, very modest indeed.

Finally, one should not forget that the end of the 1980s was a period during which steps were being taken (notably through moves to extend parental choice) to encourage schools to compete with each other for pupils. Competition *per se* does not necessarily generate increased performance. However, it may have contributed indirectly in at least two ways: first, by focusing greater attention on differences between schools in such headline statistics as the percentages of pupils obtaining five or more A–C passes; and second, by allowing schools to attempt to recruit more able pupils. However, changes in recruitment patterns alone are unlikely to produce system-wide improvements. This is a zero-sum game; one school's gain is, almost invariably, another school's loss.

The era of school improvement

The government first introduced performance tables for schools in 1992. From the detailed information we have available on schools in several LEAs, it is evident that a large number of schools responded to this development by entering their pupils for *more* examinations. Before the introduction of performance tables schools had been entering their pupils, on average, for between seven and eight subjects. Within a single year the average jumped by about one entry per pupil to between eight and nine subjects. It might be thought that there is a trade-off between the number of subjects that pupils study and their performance in each of them. In practice this does not seem to have been the case. Pupils who were entered for more examinations appear to have achieved better overall results.

The other factor operating at national level has been the increasing governmental emphasis upon school improvement and development. This started at the beginning of the 1990s with the guidance from the Department of Education and Science (DES) about school development planning (Hargreaves and Hopkins 1991). Developments since that time have included the issuing of guidance to governors about the characteristics of effective schools (Department for Education and Employment (DfEE) and Ofsted 1995), the identification of schools which were judged to have 'improved' (Ofsted 1995) and a wide array of international, national and local conferences that have focused attention on issues related to school improvement. By 1995 schools were being encouraged to set targets for their own improvement, and this trend was followed by the inclusion in 1997 of a figure relating to schools' 'improvement' in the annual performance tables.

Meanwhile individual schools have engaged, to a greater or lesser extent, in a number of other 'improvement' strategies. The most common of these has been to enter still more pupils for still more subjects. Our own research suggests that the general trend was for most schools to enter pupils for at least one more subject. Some schools, however, increased the number of exams pupils were prepared and entered for over a three- or four-year period by closer to two subjects per pupil. The introduction of a science course, which counted as two passes, will have contributed in part to this development for that group of pupils who had previously opted to take only one of the three main sciences. However, this is only part of the explanation. Some schools undoubtedly increased the load on their pupils still further.

Large numbers of schools have been engaged in recent years in identifying and targeting 'borderline' pupils for additional counselling, encouragement and, sometimes, formal tuition. Although practice has varied from school to school, many seem to have taken their definition of who the 'borderline' pupils were from the national statistics. Pupils whose grades have been predicted by their teachers to fall just short of the hurdle of five A–C passes have provided a common focus for such efforts. Again, many schools have reported that this approach 'works'. For a year cohort of 100 pupils it would only have been necessary for an extra two pupils each year from the target group to improve their performance by a grade in each of one or two subjects for a school to have kept pace with national trends. However, there are signs that this approach has been very demanding of teachers' time and that, after an initial boost to performance levels, there are diminishing returns.

There has been a good deal of interest in the extent to which variations in standards between examination boards may have contributed to the national increases. Unfortunately studies of individual schools cannot directly illuminate this issue. The influences on change outlined above would almost certainly have been sufficient to produce the larger part of the increases without any exam-board factor coming into play. Some schools have, however, reported that they deliberately changed from one board to another and that this decision contributed to improvements in their results. Such changes were, however, very selective and usually confined to one or two subjects; furthermore, these were not always the ones involving large numbers of pupils. We encountered no mass defection from one board to another, but some schools have undoubtedly shopped around, albeit on a fairly modest scale.

Nearly all schools have been involved in trying to raise expectations. In many cases this has amounted to little more than a general exhortation to staff to expect more of pupils. In rather fewer cases has it been accompanied by systematic stock-taking and the re-evaluation of existing plans and targets. Sometimes the motivation has come from within the school; on other occasions an external analysis (such as an inspection) has served as the catalyst. Changing a school's *culture*, however, is likely to require rather more concerted efforts and to take considerably longer.

Improvements have occurred among all the 1992 starting bands. However, those schools in the lowest band (0–10 per cent) have been under special pressure as so-called 'poor' results has been one of the key criteria involved in inspectors' decisions about whether a school was 'failing' and in need of 'special measures'.

Concluding comments

The proportions of pupils that schools have helped to achieve five or more A–C passes has undoubtedly risen over the last two decades. For much of this time the year-on-year improvements have been modest – sometimes barely noticeable. In more recent years, however, two 'jolts' to the system can be identified. The first surrounded the introduction of the GCSE, with its clear signal to schools that examined targets might be in prospect for (nearly) all their pupils. This 'jolt' seems to have had a considerable impact – certainly on performance and, possibly, on longer-term expectations.

The second has been of more recent provenance and has focused on the efforts schools have been making to bring about 'school improve-ment'. Schools have been undertaking a number of different activities to stimulate performance, some of them with short-term pay-offs, others with possibly longer-term ones. Undoubtedly media interest in so-called 'league tables' has been one of the external factors contributing to a changed climate of expectations within which schools have had to oper-ate. However, we should not make the mistake of thinking that the changes may be attributed to a single factor. A variety of strands, many of which were first initiated by the GCSE reforms, have combined and continued to work themselves through the system.

'Jolting' a system seems to work. However, it is in the nature of jolts that their effects will diminish over time – further strategies to stimulate progress are required. The signs are that schools have exploited most of the shorter-term opportunities. In a climate where aspirations to school improvement have become the norm, efforts to unlock how schools have been attempting to sustain improvement provide a pressing agenda.

Notes

1 Fuller technical details of the ways in which these statistics were calculated and the construction of the national database on schools can be found in Gray and Jesson (1996).
2 The correlation between the percentage of pupils in a school obtaining five or more A*–C passes in 1992 and 1995 was very high at 0.94. For the percentage obtaining five or more A–G passes the correlation between 1992 and 1995 was 0.82, while for the percentage obtaining one or more A–G passes it was 0.66.
3 The 61–100 per cent band contained a small number of schools who already had *all* their pupils securing five or more A–C passes. Clearly these schools had already reached the ceiling in terms of this particular measure and no further improvement was possible.

4 The way in which we decided to define the three different groups of schools is outlined in the footnotes to the table; doubtless other strategies could have been employed which might have yielded somewhat different results.
5 Such developments can be traced, for example, in interpretations by Her Majesty's Inspector of schools' exam results during the course of the 1980s – see Gray and Wilcox (1995) for further details – but are also evident in the ways in which LEAs were organizing and publishing their own statistics. The requirement for schools to publish their exam results in their prospectuses to parents also encouraged the use of cohort-based statistics.

 **3**

HOW TO IMPROVE: DEBATES, CONTROVERSIES AND TRADITIONS

While the pressures upon schools to improve have probably never been greater, the academic and practical resources that exist to help them are still somewhat limited. The academic communities of school effectiveness and school improvement researchers have historically been small in number, large in the areas of disagreement between opposing groups and sometimes muddled and unsystematic in their thinking. There have also been differences in methodological commitments and orientations which have not helped tasks of integration and synthesis. More recently, however, a new disciplinary grouping has begun to emerge that has sought to combine insights from both the effectiveness and improvement paradigms. It is with this latter group that our study belongs.

The school improvement tradition

The school improvement tradition of research and practice was initially a reaction to some of the top-down, externally driven changes in curriculum and organization of the 1960s (Reynolds 1988). Gathering speed in the early to mid-1980s, it celebrated a very different orientation towards 'improvement' issues – see, for example, the work of Fullan (1982). The new paradigm emphasized:

- a bottom-up orientation – school improvement should be 'owned' by the individual school and its staff;
- a concern with organizational and cultural *processes* rather than changes in the *outcomes* of the school – it was the 'journey' which mattered;
- a perspective which viewed educational outcomes as inherently problematic, requiring the discussion and adoption of goals at school level;

- a more qualitative orientation in its research methodology – the main data needed for improvement should reflect the views of the key participants;
- an interest in seeing schools as dynamic institutions, requiring extended study over time rather than the typical 'snapshots' which had characterized most cross-sectional studies; and
- a focus upon 'school culture' rather than 'school structure' as the main way of understanding the potential for school growth and development.

The involvement of the Organization for Economic Cooperation and Development (OECD) offered a major impetus to the development of this new paradigm. Between 1982 and 1986 its Centre for Educational Research and Innovation (CERI) sponsored the International School Improvement Project (ISIP). ISIP built on previous OECD/CERI initiatives such as the *Creativity of the School* project (Nisbet 1973) and the In-Service Education and Training (INSET) project (Hopkins 1987). At a time when the educational system as a whole faced not only retrenchment but also pressure for change, a project that focused on strategies for strengthening the school's capacity for problem-solving, making the school more reflexive and enhancing the teaching/learning process was seen as both important and necessary.

ISIP's approach to change differed radically from that of some of its former 'top-down' predecessors of the 1970s. The project defined 'school improvement' (van Velzen *et al*. 1985: 48) as: 'a systematic, sustained effort aimed at change in learning conditions and other related internal conditions in one or more schools, with the ultimate aim of accomplishing educational goals more effectively'. As an approach to educational change school improvement, ISIP-style, rested on a number of assumptions (Hopkins 1990; Hopkins *et al*. 1994: 69) which included the following:

- *Seeing the school as the centre of change.* External reforms needed to be sensitive to the situation in individual schools, rather than assuming that all schools were the same. It also implied that school improvement efforts needed to adopt a 'classroom-exceeding' perspective – without ignoring the classroom, they should aim to go beyond it.
- *There should be a systematic approach to change.* School improvement was seen as a carefully planned and managed process that took place over a period of several years.
- *The 'internal conditions' of schools were a key focus for change.* These included not only the teaching and learning activities used in schools but also the schools' procedures, allocation of roles and resource use.
- *Accomplishing educational goals more effectively.* Educational goals were seen as reflecting the particular mission of a school and were to be determined by what the school itself regarded as desirable.
- *The need for a multi-level perspective.* Although the school was seen as the centre of change, it did not act alone. It was embedded in an

educational system that had to work collaboratively or symbiotically for the highest degrees of quality to be achieved. This meant that the roles of teachers, heads, governors, parents, support people (advisers, higher education, consultants) and local authorities needed to be defined, harnessed and committed to the process of improvement.

• *The need for integrative implementation strategies.* This implied linkages between top-down and bottom-up approaches, remembering of course that both could apply at a number of different levels in the system. Ideally, the two would complement each other. Top-down approaches might provide such things as policy aims, an overall strategy and operational plans, while bottom-up approaches could affect such things as diagnosis, goal setting and implementation. The former provided the framework, resources and a menu of alternatives; the latter energy and school-based implementation.

• *The need for a drive towards institutionalization.* Change was only to be seen as successful when it had become part of the natural behaviour of teachers in the school – implementation by itself was not enough.

Other research studies around this time echoed and illuminated ISIP's approach. The Rand study, for example, explored some of the factors influencing change efforts (Berman and McLaughlin 1977; McLaughlin 1990), while the DESSI (Dissemination Efforts Supporting School Improvement) study carried out in the early 1980s was a similarly large-scale attempt to understand the process of innovation (Crandall *et al.* 1982; 1986). Other influential efforts to get closer to the processes of school improvement included Louis and Miles's (1992) study which took a broad look at schools involved in so-called 'effective schools' programmes, and Huberman and Miles's (1984) finer-grained study of the improvement efforts in 12 American schools.

Further examples of this more holistic and organic approach to improvement during the 1980s are to be found in various school improvement networks. These tended to be based on a particular philosophy or set of principles which constituted a sort of school improvement 'club' where the rules of admission defined a generalized approach to development work in schools. The Comer School Development Programme (Comer 1988), the Coalition of Essential Schools, which has evolved on the basis of the ideas of Ted Sizer (1989), and the League of Professional Schools led by Carl Glickman (1990) are all examples of this kind of approach. Other well-developed strategies of this type include the Learning Consortium in Toronto (Fullan *et al.* 1990; Stoll and Fink 1996), and the Improving the Quality of Education for All project in England (Hopkins *et al.* 1994; 1996).

In an influential review of these different approaches to school improvement, Joyce (1991) explored some of their strategic dimensions. He describes these as being 'doors' which can open or unlock the processes of improvement. Each of the various approaches outlined offers a different way of 'getting into' the issues. Each 'door' opens a passageway into the culture of the school. His analysis suggest five major emphases that such programmes might have:

1 *Collegiality:* the development of collaborative and professional relations within a school staff and among their surrounding communities.
2 *Research:* where a school staff studies research findings about, for example, effective schools and teaching practices or the processes of change.
3 *Action research:* where teachers collect and analyse information and data about their classrooms and schools and (sometimes and more recently) their students' progress.
4 *Curriculum initiatives:* the introduction of changes within subject areas or, as in the case of the computer and information technology, across curriculum areas.
5 *Teaching strategies:* when teachers discuss, observe and acquire a range of new teaching skills and strategies.

Joyce argues that, when pursued with sufficient vigour and enthusiasm, *all* these approaches can substantially change the culture of a school. Through careful analysis of each 'door' to school improvement, one can discover where each is likely to lead, how the passageways are connected, what proponents of any one approach can borrow from the others as well as the costs and benefits of opening any one door (or any combination) first. Single approaches, he maintains, are unlikely to be as powerful agents for school improvement as simultaneous combinations of them.

Unfortunately, this kind of synthesis has rarely happened in practice. The history of school improvement in England and Wales over the past twenty years has exhibited a dogged *singularity* of approach. School self-evaluation was popular as an agent of improvement in the late 1970s and early 1980s; the Technical and Vocational Educational Initiative appeared as a major curriculum reform in 1984; and teacher appraisal, after a long gestation period, was started in 1987. Each, in its way, was premised on the assumption that it should be given primacy in schools' efforts to change. These initiatives were closely followed, however, by the proposals of the Education Reform Act in the late 1980s and early 1990s. The main elements of this legislative programme took schools in different directions. They included a national curriculum, delegated funding, governing bodies and external inspection. These were regarded by those who introduced them as somewhat free-floating initiatives which would in combination raise standards.

There was potentially a tension here between the two traditions of school improvement. Over the past decade government has continued to initiate a series of reforms while advisers, academics and consultants have continued to advocate internal strategies such as school self-evaluation, staff development and development planning. It is only recently that efforts have been made to integrate elements of the two.

Joyce's implicit assumption was that behind each 'door' are a series of interconnecting passageways that will lead eventually to improvement. However, because of their insulated nature, most school improvement strategies fail, in practice, to a greater or lesser degree to affect the *culture* of the school. They tend to focus on individual changes, and individual teachers and classrooms, rather than on how these changes can fit in with and adapt the school's organization and ethos. As a consequence, when the doors are opened they may only lead to culs-de-sac. This difficulty partially accounts for the uneven effect of most educational reforms. To continue in this vein for a moment, it seems logical that if the problems of educational change are to be overcome, some way needs to be found of integrating organizational and curriculum change within a coherent strategy. The doors to school improvement need to be opened simultaneously or consecutively and the passageways behind them linked together.

During the past ten years a number of school improvement strategies have been developed in order to do just this – to provide, that is, the coherence and sense of strategic direction missing from previous efforts. Most of them, in line with the political pressures for decentralization, have focused on some form of intervention at the school level. Development planning, for example, provides a generic and paradigmatic illustration of a school improvement strategy, combining as it does selected curriculum change with modifications to the school's management arrangements or organization. As teachers and school leaders have struggled to take control of the process of change, such approaches have become influential (Hargreaves and Hopkins 1991; MacBeath *et al.* 1996). Increasingly, schools have been encouraged to think of school improvement as a *systematic* process involving, perhaps, a five-stage cycle that focuses directly on targets for student achievement (DfEE 1997b).

The school effectiveness tradition

A second tradition aimed at generating school improvement over the last two decades has been that of school effectiveness. It, too, had a reactive rather than a purposive beginning, being initially mainly concerned to refute the thesis that 'schools made no difference' (Coleman *et al.* 1966; Jencks *et al.* 1972) and the view that so-called background factors were dominant influences on pupils' performance (see the review in Reynolds and Cuttance 1992).

Originating in work by practitioners (Edmonds 1979) and researchers (Brookover *et al.* 1979) in the United States, and from research in the United Kingdom (see Rutter *et al.* 1979; and the review in Reynolds *et al.*

1994), a paradigm began to emerge that exhibited the following characteristics, some of which were undoubtedly strengths but others of which,
at least from the perspective of understanding improvement, were to
turn out to be limitations:

- a focus upon outcomes (and notably academic ones) which were
  accepted as being 'good';
- a concern with the study of the formal organization of schools rather
  than with their more informal processes or 'cultures';
- a focus upon the identification of the characteristics of schools that
  had already *become* effective;
- a focus upon the description of schools as static, steady-state organizations which was reflected in the use of mainly cross-sectional research
  designs; and
- a commitment to the use of quantitative methods and to the utiliza-
  tion of advanced techniques of data analysis.

Considerable strides were made during this early phase of research. However, from the point of view of understanding how school improvement
works, their contributions to understanding what is essentially a dynamic
process were inevitably limited.

None the less, from these early beginnings the shape of the school effectiveness paradigm began to be established. Subsequent work within the
paradigm during the 1980s included research on:

- 'value-added' comparisons of educational authorities in terms of their
  academic outcomes (DES 1983; 1984; Gray *et al.* 1984; Gray and Jesson
  1987; Willms 1987; Woodhouse and Goldstein 1988);
- comparisons of 'selective' school systems with comprehensive or 'all-
  ability' systems (Steedman 1980; 1983; Gray *et al.* 1983; Reynolds *et al.*
  1987);
- work into the 'scientific' properties of school effects such as their size
  and estimation (Gray 1981; 1982; Gray *et al.* 1986), the differential effectiveness of different academic sub-units or departments (Fitz-Gibbon
  1985; Willms and Cuttance 1985; Fitz-Gibbon *et al.* 1989; Fitz-Gibbon
  1996), contextual or 'balance' effects (Willms 1985; 1986; 1987) and
  differential effectiveness (Aitkin and Longford 1986; Nuttall *et al.* 1989).

Towards the end of the 1980s two landmark studies appeared. The first
was notable for the wide range of outcomes in terms of which primary
schools were assessed (including mathematics, reading, writing, attendance,
behaviour and attitudes to school), for the collection of a wide range of
data upon school processes and, for the first time in British *school* effectiveness research, a focus upon classroom processes (Mortimore *et al.* 1988).
It indicated that differences in performance between primary schools were
quite substantial.

The second study demonstrated large differences in academic effect-iveness between secondary schools (Smith and Tomlinson 1989). It also suggested that there were substantial differences in performance across different school subjects – out of 18 schools, the school that was best, for example, in maths was near the bottom in English (after allowance had been made for differences in intake).

By the beginning of the 1990s, therefore, a much clearer sense of how to evaluate schools' performances was emerging, along with a sense of some of the factors that might 'make a difference'. Since that time a variety of other issues have been explored including:

1 the stability (and instability) of school effects over time (Gray *et al.* 1995; Thomas *et al.* 1995);
2 the consistency of school effects on different outcomes – for example, in terms of different subjects or different outcome domains such as the cognitive and the affective (Goldstein *et al.* 1993; Sammons *et al.* 1993; Thomas *et al.* 1995);
3 the differential effectiveness of schools for different groups of stu-dents – for example, of different ethnic or socio-economic backgrounds or with different levels of prior attainment (Jesson and Gray 1991; Goldstein *et al.* 1993; Sammons *et al.* 1993);
4 the effects of the primary and secondary school sectors on pupils' progress over time (Goldstein 1995; Sammons *et al.* 1995);
5 the extent of variation in performances accounted for by differences in effectiveness between schools using a sophisticated statistical approach known as multi-level modelling (Gray *et al.* 1990; Daly 1991; Goldstein *et al.* 1993; Thomas and Mortimore 1996) – a number of recent studies have reported figures which suggest that between 10 per cent and 15 per cent of the variation in pupils' achievement at the secondary stages may be accounted for by educational influences, while there are some suggestions that the estimates for primary schools may be higher (Sammons *et al.* 1993; 1995);
6 the extent of departmental and subject-by-subject differences in edu-cational performance and effectiveness (Fitz-Gibbon 1991; 1992; Harris *et al.* 1995; Sammons *et al.* 1997).

At the same time the range of concerns being addressed by researchers has expanded. Recent studies have included work:

7 at the interface between school effectiveness and special educational needs, exploring how much schools can vary in their definitions, label-ling practices and teacher–pupil interactions with such children (Brown *et al.* 1996);
8 on conceptualizing the nature of the school and classroom processes within *ineffective* schools (Reynolds 1991; 1996; Stoll and Myers 1998), the main thrust of which suggests that there may be a number of

'pathologies' in such schools which make it inadvisable to study them merely from the point of view of the absence of effectiveness factors; and

9 on the potential 'context specificity' of characteristics associated with effective schools – evidence from the International School Effectiveness Research Project, a nine-nation study, strongly suggests that while some factors may 'travel' others may not (Reynolds *et al*. 1994; Reynolds and Farrell 1996).

As a result, a clearer sense of some of the key factors associated with schools' effectiveness has begun to emerge. Among the factors identified as contributing, the following have frequently been mentioned:

- The nature of the leadership provided by the headteacher. More effective schools seem to have leaders whose management style succeeds in combining the establishment of overall directions and, in that most popular of contemporary management terms, a 'mission', while simultaneously involving staff in planning the means to achieve them through their involvement in decision-making. The effective school secures a balance, then, in its management between vertical push and horizontal pull. In discussions about improvement, changing heads is undoubtedly the most frequently proposed intervention.
- The extent of academic push or 'press'. This involves having high expectations of what pupils can achieve, utilizing strategies that ensure large amounts of learning time, and focusing upon strategies (such as the setting of homework tasks) which can help to create enhanced levels of achievement.
- The use of strategies for parental involvement, both to ensure the participation of 'significant others' in children's efforts to achieve and to ensure, when needed, that parents will join the school in finding ways of supporting pupils experiencing difficulties in committing themselves to the school's goals.
- The means of securing pupil involvement, both in the classroom in terms of their learning and throughout the school in terms of participation in societies, sports teams, leadership positions, representative positions and so on.
- The fostering of organizational cohesion through the planning and coordination of school activities, through ensuring a degree of ownership of the school by the staff and through the flow of information through the school in ways which facilitate staff involvement. Such cohesion is reflected in a high degree of consistency across lessons in the same subjects, across different subjects in the same years and across different years in the pupil learning experiences on offer. As part of its approach the school is likely to support development planning and forms of professional development which involve utilizing members of staff as

'experts' who can support both their own and colleagues' needs for professional development.

Lists such as these offer some pointers to priorities for schools' improvement. However, their empirical status is sometimes debated – see Scheerens (1992) for a fuller assessment – and they are, in our view, best seen as guides for development rather than blueprints.

Some limitations of the discourse concerning 'schooling'

There is much in the school effectiveness research that resonates with contemporary educational discourse and, in particular, with the apparently increasing concern of government to intervene with a view to improvement. The emphasis in the research on the importance of leadership is one example of this kind of consonance. The Conservative government's Education Acts of 1981, 1986 and 1988 began the processes which have increasingly seen 'the school' as the main unit of policy implementation and change. The publication of schools' exam results, changes to their governance, the introduction of market-based policies to 'reward' or 'punish' schools in accordance with their popularity and the efforts to 'free' schools from LEA control all contributed to this increasing emphasis (see reviews in Hargreaves and Reynolds 1989; Ball 1990). These trends have continued in recent years and, in some respects, the focus on the school has intensified.

The traditions of school improvement and school effectiveness outlined above have clearly done something to further understanding of how improvement works in practice. Effectiveness and improvement insights undoubtedly lie at the heart of the present government's plans to improve education. Perhaps the clearest example of this kind of thinking is the way in which the White Paper *Excellence in Schools* (DES, 1997a) drew upon the philosophy and practice of 'pressure and support' (Fullan 1991; Hopkins *et al.* 1994), on the 'valued-added' analyses now axiomatic in educational effectiveness studies (Goldstein 1995; Jesson 1996; Fitz-Gibbon 1997; Sammons *et al.* 1997; Tymms 1997) and on ideas from the knowledge base of the effectiveness factors themselves (Sammons *et al.* 1994). However, the fragmented nature of much research and the sometimes oppositional nature of the separate paradigms of improvement and effectiveness (Reynolds *et al.* 1993) has meant that many 'policy-relevant' questions have not necessarily received the kind of attention they might have merited. We list below some examples where the research response to date has clearly been muted, along with some observations about how the orientations of the two research groups have contributed to or hindered the developing picture:

- *How have schools become more effective over time?* School effectiveness research has looked almost exclusively at schools that have *already* become effective. With the exception of the case studies commissioned by the National Commission on Education (1996) and the longitudinal work from the United States by Teddlie and Stringfield (1993) and Louis and Miles (1991), research on school effectiveness has not looked much at the factors that helped schools to *become* effective or to *improve*. Research on school improvement, by contrast, has looked at the issue of what generates improvement over time but has rarely sought or possessed data to show its extent or evidence about factors *associated with* the improvement.
- *How can poorly performing or ineffective schools be improved?* Unfortunately, school effectiveness research has not systematically studied these types of schools; they have largely been assumed to be mirror-images of more effective ones. There are only a few case studies and exploratory investigations (Reynolds 1991; 1996; Gray and Wilcox 1995; Stoll *et al.* 1996; Stoll and Myers 1998). The difficulties of obtaining access to these schools for research purposes, combined with the tendency of ineffective schools to drop out of research projects, have contributed to their absence in the literature. However, the main reason is simply that researchers have been insufficiently interested in them. Meanwhile, in the school improvement tradition ineffective schools have also failed to get much mention. Again, there have been several reasons. Part of the problem has been a 'one size fits all' orientation. Improvement mechanisms have been conceived independently of schools' levels of effectiveness, their culture, their socio-economic context or their 'improvement trajectories'.
- *What do schools look like as they improve and change over time?* Given the formidable problems of data collection, school effectiveness studies have usually focused upon the passage of a single age cohort through their schools. They have therefore only looked at schools in a 'snapshot' or cross-sectional manner. Where additional cohorts have been utilized, this has normally been to generate reliability ratings or consistency estimates in relation to the first or 'prime' cohort. In the school improvement literature, by contrast, the oft-stated belief that change is a long-term process has not often been associated with research designs that were long-term in nature.
- *Which particular strategies of school development or school improvement are most effective in changing school/classroom processes and outcomes?* Historically, the school effectiveness tradition has had little to say about these matters because the sorts of school improvement strategies that have been utilized in schools (particular types of school development planning, for example, or the use of particular kinds of 'off-the-shelf' improvement designs) have either not featured or featured only marginally in the data on school organizational factors usually collected.

Meanwhile, in the school improvement tradition, there has been a notable reluctance to test out the effects of improvement programmes. Part of the reason for this has been philosophical and related to the difficulty those engaged in school improvement have had in agreeing upon criteria through which to judge 'effectiveness'. Where evidence on the effects of particular strategies has been collected this has tended to be confined to the 'micro level'; the systematic evaluation of different overarching strategies has either been taken for granted or, for a mixture of reasons, ignored.

While there is fairly widespread agreement that these factors are important, debates none the less continue about the underlying evidence for them and their epistemological status (see, for example, critiques in Barber and White 1997; and Slee *et al.* 1998). In the areas of school effectiveness and improvement it seems unwise to assert too forcibly what works.

The American contribution

Research in both traditions and on both sides of the Atlantic has undoubtedly been limited by the kinds of difficulties outlined above. However, the last few years have seen some attempts to move forward, both intellectually and practically. In the USA, for example, the Teddlie and Stringfield (1993) study in Louisiana involved the long-term study of the 'natural history' of a number of elementary schools of different levels of effectiveness and serving different socio-economic contexts. The research included the identification of 'improving' and 'declining' schools as well as some attempt to explore factors associated with their change.

Within the improvement tradition, meanwhile, Louis and Miles's (1992) picture of urban high schools involved the exploration of a number of factors that led schools to report improved performance on a variety of different outcomes (including pupils' attitudes and achievements as well as staff morale). The research used a methodology that involved case studies of schools and a larger survey of some 200 which had adopted so called 'effective schools' programmes. The study is limited, however, by the extent to which it relied largely on principals' reports to judge how much 'improvement' had occurred. Given the personal commitments that the principals would have had to make in order to become involved in these programmes, it seems highly likely that they would have been predisposed to report that they had been (more or less) successful, partly at least by virtue of their adoption of the programmes.

A third, and equally forward-looking, American study is Rosenholtz's (1989) account of the characteristics of schools which she characterized as 'stuck' or 'moving'. However, while the study is rich on factors potentially associated with change, it is difficult to establish the extent and scale of change across the sample.

More recent research has begun which could begin to answer some of the policy and practice questions noted above. Combining methodologies and utilizing data upon a multiplicity of school factors that relate to programme characteristics and school organization, cohort-based studies have been concerned to evaluate the US federal government's 'Special Strategies' study of school improvement for schools educating disadvantaged children (Stringfield *et al.* 1994; 1997). Similar work has also been in progress in Memphis, where the local school board and university are currently taking part in an ambitious evaluation of a range of school-based improvement strategies such as Slavin's (1996) 'Roots and Wings' scheme. This research involves a cohort of students who are themselves being assessed as they move through school, along with the collection of a wide range of data on the schools' contexts, the programmes' characteristics and the 'implementation' and/or 'institutionalization' of the programmes themselves. Meanwhile, in Louisiana, Freeman and Teddlie (1997) have been conducting work on the characteristics of three categories of schools ('improvers', 'decliners' and 'stable') selected on the basis of their performance over time in the state-wide testing programme.

The response of practitioners to the British research

Similar attempts to merge research traditions have been taking place in the United Kingdom. There is some evidence, however, to suggest that practitioners are impatient with those labels beloved of the research community that have functioned to mark out, delimit and differentiate research communities (Stoll and Fink 1996). Consequently, many LEA initiatives have 'borrowed' from both the effectiveness and improvement traditions at the same time, 'blending' insights as circumstances have dictated (see, for example, Myers 1996; Reynolds *et al.* 1996; Stoll and Thomson 1996).

At the same time a large number of 'centres' or 'institutes' concerned with aspects of school improvement have been set up. These tend to involve networks of practitioners, policy-makers and researchers interacting in a 'problem-oriented' way. Examples of this kind of development can be seen in the activities of centres at the University of Nottingham, which is piloting some of Slavin's (1996) work on remedial reading, the International School Effectiveness and Improvement Centre at the University of London Institute of Education which is working on several fronts (Mortimore 1998), the University of Bath (Harris *et al.* 1995), the University of Newcastle upon Tyne which is attempting to develop 'high-reliability' schools (Stringfield and Reynolds 1996) and a network in Cambridge where pupils' perspectives on change have been given particular attention (Rudduck *et al.* 1996). Other researchers have been evaluating the increasing involvement of LEA personnel in school improvement

(Coleman and Riley 1995; Southworth and Sebba 1997) as well as the impact of the funds made available to schools and LEAs by the DfEE for school improvement (Sebba *et al.* 1998). Meanwhile, LEAs as diverse as Sheffield and Shropshire have been setting up their own in-house centres and produced targeted reports for teachers on the improvement process (see, for example, Hedger and Jesson 1998).

This 'merger' of concerns, traditions and methods being attempted by researchers and practitioners in the UK has also been evident in the activities of bodies with an interest in policy development. For example, Ofsted (1994) has reported on the characteristics of a small number of 'improving' schools and committed itself to the motto 'improvement through inspection' (Earley *et al.* 1996; Wilcox and Gray 1996).

More recently, there has been increased interest in the problems facing schools in trouble. The DfEE has commissioned some case studies of schools emerging from so-called 'special measures' (Mortimore 1996), while other studies have looked at the role of LEAs in supporting such schools (Riley and Rowles 1997; Whatford 1998). The most substantial study to date in this area, however, has been undertaken by Ofsted (1997a), which also looked at some of the characteristics of schools that have been 'making satisfactory or good progress' to get out of special measures. Some common elements in the experiences of these schools have included: ensuring strong leadership is provided (which has often involved the appointment of a new headteacher); taking vigorous action to improve the quality of teaching, pupils' progress and levels of attainment; producing and implementing school policy documents and schemes of work; taking immediate steps to improve pupils' behaviour; preparing action plans which contain focused success criteria and clear targets; getting governing bodies to work more effectively; being well supported by their LEAs; and receiving additional financial support from their LEA (or from the Funding Agency for Schools).

In sum, there are various promising signs that both researchers and practitioners have begun to address some of the very practical issues which arise when school improvement is attempted.

The new paradigm

In retrospect, it is clear that there has been a gradual drawing together of the concerns and approaches of the two disciplines of 'school effectiveness' and 'school improvement', spurred by the existence of practitioners and policy-makers increasingly using both bodies of knowledge to improve their practice. This process of merging traditions has gone furthest in the USA but is also clearly in evidence in the UK. What is currently beginning to emerge, then, is a new paradigm of effectiveness/improvement concerns that represents a distinctively new way of focusing upon the practical problems of improving schools – see Gray *et al*. (1996b), Reynolds *et al*. (1996) and Stoll and Fink (1996) for further elaboration of the paradigm.

Work within this 'new' paradigm can be characterized in the following terms:

- More projects are adopting a 'mixed' methodological orientation, in which bodies of quantitative and qualitative data are amalgamated to assess programmes' qualities and effects; the new paradigm employs whichever methods seem best fitted to the problem(s) under study.
- In marked contrast to earlier work on school improvement during the 1980s, the learning level, the instructional behaviours of teachers and the classroom itself are increasingly being targeted for explicit programme attention.
- The new paradigm aims to pull a variety of 'levers' to influence what goes on in schools; increasingly the concern has shifted away from what is a 'good' school to how one makes a school 'good'.
- There is simultaneous interest in both the processes of schools and the outcomes they generate.
- Finally, there is some recognition that schools' development needs to be charted over the medium to long term.

The key challenges for the Improving Schools Project

In designing the study reported in this book we have kept many of these considerations to the fore. We believe that the resulting study is distinctive in at least two respects: first, because it employs both qualitative and quantitative methods to chart and understand the mechanisms of improvement, drawing on a wide variety of participants in the schooling process (including heads, deputies, teachers, pupils, chairs of governors, secretaries, caretakers and other support staff); and second, through its use of knowledge gained from both the school effectiveness *and* school improvement paradigms to identify factors that might have contributed to the change and improvement process.

In thinking about what to study, we have looked at three literatures in some detail: that on school effectiveness factors (see, for example, reviews in Mortimore *et al*. 1988; Reynolds and Cuttance 1992; Scheerens 1992; Creemers 1994; and Reynolds *et al*. 1996); that on mechanisms contributing to school improvement discussed in the school development literature (see, for example, reviews in Fullan 1991; 1992; Hargreaves and Hopkins 1991; Cuttance 1994; Hopkins *et al*. 1994; Stoll and Fink 1994); and that from practitioners reflecting current notions of 'good (professional) practice' (see, for example, Brighouse 1991; and Ofsted 1994). Our reading of these various literatures presents us, therefore, with questions in a number of areas which we have chosen to group under the following headings:

1 *Short-term tactics.* Schools may have employed a variety of approaches to get things 'moving'. Have exam syllabuses been changed? Have schools changed exam boards? Have a higher proportion of the age cohort been entered for public exams? Have more pupils been entered for more exams? Have certain pupil groups (such as those with special needs, boys or girls, ethnic minorities, children from disadvantaged backgrounds) been targeted? Were pupils on the borderline of particular exam 'thresholds' (for example, five 'good' passes) given extra counselling or encouragement?

2 *School personnel.* Did key leaders, teachers or support staff arrive or move on during the period of change? If so, in what ways did those who arrived or left differ? What policy changes ensued?

3 *School development/improvement strategies.* Did 'improving' schools focus upon particular goals (or issues), perhaps at the expense of others? Did they develop specific strategies or mechanisms for improvement planning? How far were these generated internally and how far did they involve external support? Were data on (or assessments of) the 'performance' of the school as a whole, individual departments or individuals influential at particular times? To what extent was a deliberate effort made to create greater 'ownership' of the change programme? Was priority given to professional development initiatives? In what ways was school improvement resourced, supported and rewarded?

4 *The context of change.* Were there any particular events or occasions when the school's performance was in the public spotlight? Were any 'external reviews' (of either a formal or informal nature) undertaken? What influence did national reforms have? Were there any factors which enhanced local competition between schools? Were there any significant changes in pupil recruitment to the school? Have community expectations changed at all? What has been the influence of any LEA-led initiatives?

5 *The experience of change.* How have members of the school reacted to the changes over the last few years? Are they aware that their institution is improving, deteriorating or standing still? To what extent are such perceptions shared across the institution? Were there particular points at which morale was weakened or strengthened? How do participants themselves explain past changes? How far do they envisage further changes?

As we proceeded, this initial checklist of possible questions began to be modified and extended in the light of our emerging understanding. We also started to realize that we would not be able, within the constraints of a single study, to probe all of them in equal depth. The resulting range of potentially important factors was both extensive and at times, daunting. It is easy enough to identify some of the weaknesses of previous research efforts, quite another to attempt to address them in ways which are convincing. Their limitations may have partly resulted from the absence of an 'integrating' tradition, but they are also likely to have been constrained by practicalities. Indeed, the latter may well have been the more influential. It is to some of the details of the study we eventually designed and implemented, therefore, that we turn in the following chapters.

 **4**

FRAMEWORKS FOR JUDGING
SCHOOL IMPROVEMENT

'School improvement' is a fuzzy term, widely employed to cover a multitude of changes in schools. What, then, should count as 'school improvement'? And, if some worthwhile conceptualizations can be agreed, how might one begin to operationalize them?

Four ways of gauging improvement

To date we have identified four main ways in which people attempt to assess the extent of school improvement. Probably the most frequently adopted approach is for someone in a school (usually the head or a senior member of staff) to relate what has happened in their own words. Such accounts typically start with a brief sketch of how things were at some previous time and then provide a more or less detailed step-by-step story of what has happened since then.

In their study of urban high schools, Louis and Miles (1992) adopted a more systematic version of this approach. They asked headteachers, all of whom were now three years into 'effective school' programmes, to estimate how much change had taken place in their schools as a result of their participation. They used a number of different outcome measures, including changes in such things as staff morale and pupil achievement. They then tried to relate the heads' views about these changes to various other factors on which they had collected information.

A third approach involves judgements by people who are external to the school about how much change has taken place. Inspectors who inspect and then, at some later date, reinspect a school are currently being asked to form views about the extent of 'improvement' which has occurred in the intervening period (Ofsted 1996, 1997b).

Finally, there has been some concern to consider the extent of 'improvement' in terms of so-called 'harder' measures such as exam and test results. An explicit focus on outcomes is a fairly recent development but, with the advent of national frameworks for testing, interest in such strategies has undoubtedly been growing.

All four of these approaches need, of course, to be viewed within the contexts within which 'school improvement' occurs. A school which has committed itself of its own volition to 'improvement' is likely to be looking for evidence that it has succeeded. Such a school might also have joined an 'improvement' project co-ordinated by its LEA or a group of researchers. Such actions again create the expectation that if the school comes up with appropriate strategies and implements them, 'improvement' will have taken place. The claims to have improved are likely to be strong. Securing a measure of distance from them, therefore, is likely to be difficult.

Building in the element of time

The biggest problem for anyone who is interested in assessing school improvement is that it takes place over time. Any statement about 'improvement' contains an implicit time dimension because it involves, at a minimum, comparisons between at least two points in time. Such statements also incorporate assumptions about how improvement is best measured.

The time dimension also influences what is meant by improvement. For example, when the time-frame is relatively short (a term or two) it is usually changes in such things as teachers' attitudes which are being referred to. Changes in pupil outcome measures are likely to take longer – a pupil who enters a secondary school which has initiated a process of improvement does not, after all, secure any exam results until some five years later. If it takes up to five years to collect relevant data on a single cohort of pupils passing through school, then cumulative evidence on several cohorts will take longer still.[1] It is not difficult to see why there have, to date, been few long-term studies of improvement.

The time dimension is frustrating for policy-makers and practitioners, both of whom may be anxious to check that their investments in change have paid off. It is at least as frustrating for researchers because longitudinal or quasi-longitudinal studies, which follow up cohorts of pupils over time, are among the most difficult, expensive and time-consuming to conduct. It is scarcely surprising, therefore, that nearly every study in this area (including our own) has had to make compromises in how the time dimension of improvement is handled.

Key questions about schools' performance

There are basically three ways in which a school's performance may be judged. Historically, questions about how schools are performing in relation to national standards have dominated. Questions about how a school performs in relation to national averages, however, have never been of more than passing interest to researchers of school effectiveness.

A second set of questions asks how 'effectively' schools have performed with the pupils they have. Essentially this approach depends on comparing schools on a like-with-like basis. Debates about what 'like-with-like' comparisons involve have not been fully resolved, but there is something approaching a consensus about the basic strategies – see Gray and Wilcox (1995) for a fuller discussion. Schools with disadvantaged or low-attaining intakes are only usefully compared with schools with similarly disadvantaged or low-attaining intakes. In short, 'effectiveness' is a relative concept whose extent can only be established by empirical investigation. The 'most effective' schools are the ones whose pupils progress the farthest from where they started – the ones which, in the current jargon, 'add the most value'.

Techniques for establishing schools' effectiveness have become increasingly sophisticated in recent years. Paradoxically, however, the kinds of statements about schools' performances which researchers now feel it is legitimate to make have become increasingly straightforward. The great majority of schools are of average effectiveness – they are performing, in other words, at around the levels one would predict from knowledge of their intakes. Only a minority of schools can justifiably be described as performing significantly better or worse than predicted. Consequently, three straightforward categories seem to suffice to cover most schools: they are either 'more effective', of 'average effectiveness' or 'less effective'.

The third (and most recent) set of questions relates to 'improvement'. We have already hinted that this notion is, in our view, often used rather loosely. Our concern here is to establish some criteria which might need to be met for it to be useful to talk of an 'improving' school. In Figure 4.1, therefore, we have presented some hypothetical possibilities.

Figure 4.1(a) shows a pretty straightforward situation. Data on outcomes have been assembled over a five-year period. For the purposes of the example, three different schools are assumed to have had the same results in 1990 but then proceeded along different 'improvement' paths over the following four years; in each case the general trend has been upwards and in relatively equal steps. However, while all three have clearly been improving their results, it seems useful to add some commentary about the rate of improvement: relative to each other one has improved 'rapidly', one more 'steadily' and one more 'slowly'.

Figure 4.1(b) presents the trajectories for two further schools which are more difficult to describe. Although they have eventually reached roughly

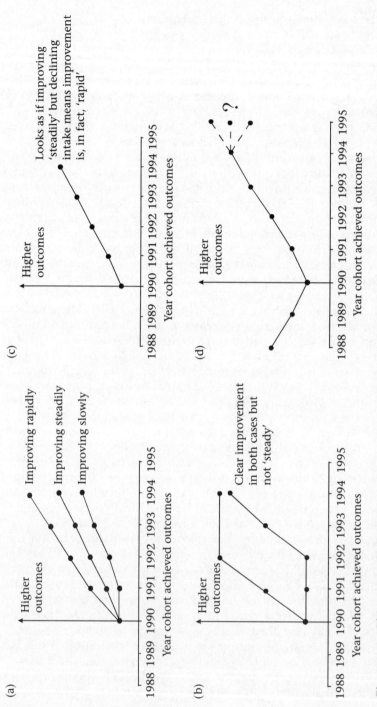

Figure 4.1 The interpretation of improvement trajectories for separate cohorts of pupils: (a) intake stays constant, interpretation straightforward; (b) intake stays constant, interpretation problematic; (c) intake declines over time, interpretation needs care; (d) trends over longer term, interpretation problematic

the same positions as the 'rapid' improvers, their routes have differed. They could both justifiably be referred to as 'improving' schools but tapping into the stages at which improvement has been occurring is more problematic – in one case one would need to have been there at the start, in the other rather later on.

The performance of a further school is described in Figure 4.1(c). At first glance its improvement trajectory seems to correspond to that of the 'steady' improver in Figure 4.1(a). However, the performance of the pupils when they entered this school has, in fact, been declining slowly over the same period. When this is factored into the analysis, this school turns out to be a 'rapid' improver. While many schools have intakes which remain stable over time, there are undoubtedly others whose intakes fluctuate quite considerably from one year to the next. Sensitivity to this dimension is crucial to an adequate assessment of performance.

This example makes explicit what has been merely been stated as an assumption in Figures 4.1(a) and 4.1(b) – namely, that comparisons of schools' rates of improvement can only meaningfully be conducted when intakes stay constant from one year to the next. Most analyses of school improvement *assume* this to be the case. Our evidence indicates that, for a very substantial minority of schools, this is not a good working hypothesis. Data about year-on-year changes need to be collected and routinely taken into account.[2]

The importance of taking the longer view is underlined in the case of the school in Figure 4.1(d). Between 1990 and 1994 this school also seems to have been a 'rapid' improver. However, it is clear that this interpretation would need to be heavily qualified if one had had evidence on its performance in either of the two preceding years (1988 and 1989) and might possibly need to be qualified in a subsequent one (1995). Indeed, in one variant the school's 1995 results were scarcely better than those for 1988.

Historically, researchers have mostly been interested in differences in schools' *effectiveness*. They have given scant attention to differences in schools' *rates of improvement*, often treating these as unwelcome intrusions upon an otherwise stable picture (see Gray *et al.* 1995). One further modification to the notion of school improvement is required, however, before the two research traditions can be appropriately integrated.

The two dimensions of effectiveness and improvement

It is convenient to refer to schools' 'rates of improvement' as the primary concern of the present study but what is really of interest are estimates of the schools' 'rates of improvement in their *effectiveness*'. The 'improving' school, in other words, is the one which secures year-on-year improvements in the outcomes of successive cohorts of 'similar' pupils.[3]

Let us assume, for the sake of this example, that a school is of average effectiveness for a particular cohort of pupils. To begin to count as an 'improving' school it must improve upon this performance the next year by adding a little more value to its second cohort of pupils than it did to its first. In the year after that it needs to take another step, adding still more value to its third cohort of pupils than it managed for the second; and so on. In other words, if it started out as being of merely 'average' effectiveness, then one would expect it, a number of years later, to be either identified as a school of 'above average' effectiveness or a good deal closer to being identified with such schools than it was before. It is a moot point over how many cohorts it would have to improve to count as an 'improving' school. A minimum of three cohorts is required to establish a trend; five would be better to ensure that the trajectory was becoming established and more would be desirable.

In the past school effectiveness researchers tended to focus on what made one school 'more effective' than another, while school improvement researchers tended to look at what made one school 'improve' faster than another. In our view these two perspectives need to be integrated into a single framework, and this is what we have attempted to do in Figure 4.2.

Just three schools have been identified in Figure 4.2. Each of these is initially of differing 'effectiveness'. Their 'effectiveness' is established by relating the schools' outcomes to the prior attainments and/or other aspects of their pupils' backgrounds which influence pupils' progress.

First, an estimate can be established for the schools' initial effectiveness in relation to their year 1 cohorts; this is all most studies of school effectiveness would have available. Our concern, however, has been to look at changes in schools' effectiveness over time. For this purpose further estimates of effectiveness for subsequent cohorts are required, covering the cohorts of pupils who subsequently passed through the schools in years 2, 3, 4 and 5. As a result, no fewer than five estimates of schools' effectiveness are available.

The next stage is to try to establish whether there are any trends in the estimates of schools' effectiveness across the five cohorts. In a school which was 'improving rapidly' in its effectiveness the estimate for the second cohort would be higher than that for the first cohort, the estimate for the third higher than the second, for the fourth higher than the third, and for the fifth higher than the fourth. Furthermore, when one compared the estimates for the first cohort with those for the fifth one would expect the latter to be higher, although by how much is a matter for empirical estimation. What is true for schools of 'above average' effectiveness is equally true for schools whose initial effectiveness was 'average' or 'below average'.

Extending this approach to the other improvement trajectories, one can see that a school where the estimates of effectiveness went down for

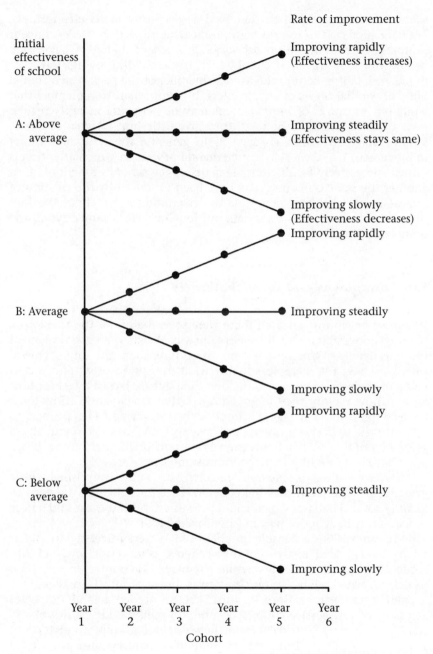

Figure 4.2 Combining the dimensions of effectiveness and improvement

successive cohorts could be described as declining in its effectiveness. We have preferred to use the term 'improving slowly', however, since it captures better, to our mind, schools' *experiences* of change. As Figure 4.2 demonstrates, however, a school which is merely 'improving slowly' is, in practice, falling behind the average member of the pack which started out with similar levels of effectiveness. It is important to remember that while our measures of improvement may be behaving in fairly regular ways from one year to the next, they give little hint of what processes schools may have been engaged in to generate them. In one school improvement may be a steady incremental process in which attention is turned successively to different elements of the school's functioning. In another the same outcomes may have been produced by the creation of a clear break with past practices. Understanding more about the lead times for innovations is essential, and looking behind and beyond the numbers still more so.

Some unknowns and some challenges

When we began our research there were several areas of the framework outlined above about which we were unclear. We knew a good deal about the 'effectiveness' dimension but almost nothing about the 'improvement' side. We knew, for example, roughly what the spread of schools was in terms of their effectiveness at any one time but we lacked a feel for how far and how rapidly they might improve that effectiveness. How long, for example, would it take a school of 'below average' effectiveness to pull into the pack or for a school of 'average' effectiveness to pull ahead of it? Identifying such schools is an important preliminary to establishing what has brought about the improvement.

When we turned to previous research, we found surprisingly little evidence to help us. A pressing concern, therefore, became the need to identify some databases which could help us establish the size and nature of variations in schools' 'rates of improvement'.

By the mid-1990s a sizeable number of LEAs were interested in undertaking 'value-added' analyses of their schools' exam results and had consequently begun to assemble relevant databases. The number in a position to help us when we began our study was, however, much smaller.

There were several reasons for this. First, we needed data on outcomes across several successive cohorts. Second, for methodological reasons we were only interested in databases where one could build up pictures of schools' performance from data on individual pupils. Third, we needed information which would allow us to contextualize the performance of each pupil (measures of prior attainment and social background being the most obvious candidates). However, by the time we had explored LEAs' willingness to participate in a research project of the kind we envisaged, the small number we believed were in a position to meet our basic requirements had been reduced to just a handful. At this stage pragmatic considerations concerning geographical accessibility and interest in the research also began to loom large.

Choosing LEAs and establishing data-sets

Simple analyses of the 'raw' statistics can throw up some interesting questions but they tell one little or nothing about changes in schools' 'effectiveness' because no information about schools' intakes is available. A school might have been improving to some extent merely because it was attracting a more able intake. We needed to work with schools and LEAs where data on pupil intakes at entry and exam outcomes at 16 could be matched up for individual pupils. In addition, we needed to be able to do this for a number of cohorts of pupils. We were fortunate, therefore, to have had access to several LEAs which had been involved in value-added work for a number of years. Hardly any of these contacts, however, had suitable records which either stretched back far enough for our purposes or offered the prospect of doing so.

Our strategy, therefore, was to identify LEAs which we knew had detailed information on their schools' intakes and GCSE exam outcomes over a number of years based on individual pupil records. In the event we found only a few and eventually were pleased to secure just three. These allowed us to develop sounder, value-added estimates of rates of improvement based on the statistical technique known as multi-level modelling. However these data-sets also had some drawbacks. They were, of course, limited to just three LEAs; while none of these was obviously 'untypical' of LEAs more generally, they clearly did not amount to a nationally representative sample. Furthermore, each LEA had adopted different procedures for collecting its core data; consequently the evidence could not be pooled into a single data-set for the purposes of analysis. There was one other particular feature of our research design (and our consequent choice of LEAs) which needs to be emphasized at this point. The schools we were studying were all engaged in school improvement to a greater or lesser extent when we visited them. Their efforts were, however, largely of their own making. While they sometimes engaged in improvement projects these rarely, if ever, became the main engine behind the change processes. Our study, therefore, offers some insights into the limits and possibilities of what Teddlie and Stringfield (1993) would call 'naturally occurring' improvements. It remains an open question whether more dramatic changes could be secured by external interventions.

Estimates of improvement derived from the multi-level model

We pioneered a multi-level analysis of schools' rates of improvement using a data-set from one LEA which contained information about individual pupils' prior attainments and gender as well as their exam results. In this particular LEA data were available for five separate cohorts of pupils passing through well over 30 different secondary schools. Further details about this analysis, which was the first to incorporate an 'improvement' dimension into estimates of schools' performance, have been published elsewhere (see Gray *et al.* 1996a). The approach thereby generated was then followed, as far as possible, in relation to the analyses of data from secondary schools' in two other LEAs.[4]

In general, the analyses replicated the findings of earlier research regarding the amounts of variance potentially attributable to schools. The estimates each data-set produced concerning the ranges of effectiveness between schools were entirely in line with what earlier research had led us to expect. The most striking finding to emerge from the analysis, however, related to the breakdown of this variance. Within the timeframe of the five cohorts of pupils around four-fifths of the variance was found to be associated with the effectiveness dimension, leaving only one-fifth for the improvement dimension. In other words, schools which were identified as more effective one year continued to be more effective in subsequent years; conversely, schools which were identified as less effective one year continued to be less effective in subsequent years. Differences between schools in their effectiveness simply swamped any changes in effectiveness (upwards or downwards).

The multi-level modelling also offered some insights into the kind of typology we had adopted to categorize schools. Earlier research had established that schools could only usefully be divided into three levels of 'effectiveness' – 'above average', 'average' and 'below average' (see, for example, Goldstein and Spiegelhalter 1996; Thomas and Mortimore 1996). Similarly, it was clear from the data relating to estimates of improvement from the multi-level model that only three levels of 'improvement' could usefully be distinguished – 'rapid', 'steady' and 'slow'. It needs to be remembered, of course, in this context, that a 'slow' improver is one which is falling behind other schools; it may possibly be deteriorating in terms of its actual performance levels from one year to the next. In practice only a very few of the schools which we dubbed 'slow' improvers fell into this position; most were simply lagging behind. Combining the two dimensions, therefore, produced the nine-category framework summarized in Figure 4.2 ('above average' effectiveness and improving 'rapidly', 'above average' effectiveness and improving 'steadily' and so on through to 'below average' effectiveness and improving 'slowly').

We considered further refinements to the model but decided that these would be unhelpful.[5] A nine-category framework seems to provide a useful working description of the estimates emerging from the multi-level model. It is, however, something of a compromise and ignores the evidence, for example, that a small number of schools were differentially effective with different kinds of pupils. Our decision to focus on a single 'improvement' outcome for each school was, at this stage, largely pragmatic. The first challenge was to explore the simple framework; refinements to it could come later.

While stability seems to be an enduring feature of school systems, some instability must also be present for school improvement to take place. We found that there was a minority of schools (around a quarter) which were clearly changing their positions. These were divided fairly equally between those which were improving in their effectiveness and those declining. In both cases, however, the actual number of schools falling into these categories in any one LEA was small (see Gray *et al.* 1996a: Figure 3); the number which appeared to be changing their positions in a *consistent* way from one year to the next was even smaller. None the less, there were a few on which to focus our research.

We were able to estimate rates of change over time. Among the more 'rapid' improvers this averaged around one grade (one exam point) in one subject per pupil per year. In other words, if a typical pupil started out with six grade C passes in the first year the typical pupil in the next cohort in the same school would have secured five grade Cs and a grade B and in the third cohort this would have risen to 4 grade Cs and two grade Bs and so on.[6] Among the 'slow' improvers the year-on-year changes tended in a downward direction, although again it needs to be understood that the 'raw' statistics might merely have indicated that they were apparently standing still.

A further finding related to the ease with which schools were able to move from one level of effectiveness to another (say from being clearly of 'below average' effectiveness to 'average' effectiveness). Up to three years of continuous improvement seems to have represented a good run for a school before it 'reached a plateau' or 'hit the wall'. For a school to succeed in moving up a level of effectiveness, however, required slightly more than this. Four or five years of sustained improvements were necessary. In practice, very few of the schools we studied managed to change groups in this way. Even our five-year time-frame was probably too short and the rates of improvement of even the 'rapid' improvers were not quite fast enough.

Concluding comments

In short, three or four years of continuous improvement seems to represent a good run. For a school to change its 'label' (or to come near to doing so) by moving from one level of effectiveness to another represents a considerable challenge and typically takes another year or two.

The existence of some schools which are consistently changing in their effectiveness over time provides an important first step in the quest for greater understanding of the dynamics of improvement. However, the relative contributions of the effectiveness and improvement dimensions (and, in particular, the extent to which the former dominates the latter) suggest that the identification of key correlates of improvement, which hold up across numbers of schools, will be problematic.

In formulating the next stage of our research we found it necessary to keep two concerns in mind at the same time. We were undoubtedly interested in whether there were any processes of school improvement which transcended circumstances and contexts. But first we needed to get closer to what had actually been happening in the schools. To do so meant that we had to change research styles. It is to our attempts to reconstruct schools' 'natural histories' of change that the next part of this study is devoted. For this purpose we selected just 12 schools on different improvement trajectories from across the three LEAs for more intensive study.

Notes

1 In the case of the present study the prior attainment data on the early cohorts of pupils were first collated in the mid to late 1980s. Clearly this study was only possible because we were able to retrieve the information some eight to ten years later.

2 See Gray *et al.* (1996a) for a fuller picture of the extent to which the measured performance of schools' intakes can fluctuate from year to year.

3 In practice, the task of ensuring that cohorts of pupils are 'comparable' is normally achieved through the use of statistical procedures using measures such as prior attainment and social background as controls.

4 The schools in the three LEAs have been promised that their results will be treated in confidence. The decision (partly made in response to comments from referees of the original research proposal and partly because of initial difficulties with data collection in the second LEA) to explore improvement issues in several LEAs presented a number of problems. In the second and third LEAs, for example, data on individual pupils was available for *four* cohorts rather than five. There were also some other important differences. In the second LEA a measure of prior attainment was also available along with information about gender. In the third LEA, however, only measures relating to pupils' social backgrounds (rather than prior attainments) were available. Similar data had proved reasonably robust in earlier work, had been shown to have good explanatory power and were reasonably extensive in terms of the aspects of pupils' backgrounds covered. One obvious consequence of the decision to work with datasets from three separate LEAs, however, was that the factors which generated the 'effectiveness' and 'improvement' estimates in each LEA differed. When

analyses were undertaken later on in the research to try to establish some of the correlates of improvement, the analyses were consequently confined to a simple description of their position within the effectiveness/improvement typology. Clearly it would have been preferable to employ common measures of intake characteristics across all three LEAs. With the advent of National Curriculum testing this will, in due course, become possible. However, with the matching of data for individual pupils at Key Stages 2 and 4 still on the horizon the time when data-sets comparable to those employed here can be analysed is still some years away.

5 After the statistical analyses had been completed, each of the schools was assigned to one of the categories outlined in Figure 4.2. Given that the estimates had been derived from three different data-sets an element of judgement was required here. Furthermore, in some categories of the effectiveness/ improvement framework the choice of specific schools for further study was distinctly limited for two reasons. First, hardly any schools were found to be clearly identified members of the category (this was a particular problem with the above average effectiveness/rapidly improving group). Second, there were sometimes good reasons why a school did not want to participate in this necessarily demanding phase of the research (participation in a forthcoming Ofsted inspection being the most obvious one).

6 Of course, no single summary exam statistic can capture the various dimensions of schools' performances. As the schools in our three LEAs all took the full range of pupils we opted for the exam points score, which awards a score for every grade and, in our view, most appropriately captures a school's efforts to improve the quantity of exam passes its pupils secured as well as the quality. In general, we have found that the main outcome measures were highly correlated (0.85 and above). Our decision to employ the total points score was also based on the fact that this was one of the most commonly used measures in each of the three LEAs and also the only one (other than the five A–C hurdle) which provided a common focus across the three LEAs. The highly correlated nature of the different exam measures suggests that we would have secured similar results if we had employed other measures instead but does not, of course, rule out the possibility that our choice favoured some schools at the expense of others.

▶ ▶ ▷ Part II

CASE STUDIES OF SCHOOLS

The first phase of our research provided us with detailed knowledge about how the schools in the three LEAs had performed over the last four or five years, in terms of both effectiveness and improvement. Our next concern was to try to understand what had produced the changes. We quickly realized, however, that the methodological challenges we faced were formidable.

The most obvious of these were the constraints imposed by the time dimension itself. Our knowledge of the schools' performances was firmly based but none the less constructed after the event. If we could have been confident that schools which were on 'rapidly' improving trajectories would continue to improve in subsequent years then we might have chosen to study their experiences in 'real' time. Unfortunately, it was clear from the evidence we had already assembled that hardly any schools continued to improve inexorably from year to year – a five-year run was quite exceptional. The option of tapping into ongoing 'improvement' processes was therefore available only in some cases.

A second concern was that the resources available to us for fieldwork were relatively limited. We were faced with a choice between studying all the schools in the three LEAs (assuming they would cooperate) fairly superficially (through, say, a day visit followed up by a questionnaire to teachers) or a much smaller number (around a dozen) in greater depth.

A third problem was that we lacked a clear set of signals from earlier research about what precisely to study. We identified two competing strands in the earlier literature: one drew attention to the broad themes (of planning, ethos and management, for example) which could be expected to affect the majority of schools undergoing change; the other placed greater emphasis on the context-specific, sometimes idiosyncratic nature of the change process in particular schools. Elements of both approaches chimed with our own experiences and inclinations.

Finally, and perhaps most importantly, we were uncertain how far the 'natural histories' of change in individual institutions could be *retrospectively* reconstructed. To what extent did present events colour previous ones? And how far could memories be relied on? Encouragingly, our pilot work suggested that *some* reconstruction was possible; it also suggested, however, that some individuals might engage in greater reinterpretation than others.

With the benefit of hindsight, it is clear that different researchers attribute different importance to these various constraints and that it is likely to be some time before an accepted way of undertaking this kind of study emerges. Eventually, bearing in mind the concern that we should sample schools across more than one LEA, we decided to select a small number of institutions (12 in all across the three LEAs) on different improvement trajectories (judged in terms of the framework presented in Figure 4.2) for more intensive study, rather than spread ourselves more thinly.[1]

During the first stage, two members of the research team were assigned to build up a picture of each institution's 'natural history' of change using a variety of sources of evidence but giving particular primacy to data gathered from semi-structured interviews with a broad range of staff involved in each school.[2] They visited each school on a number of separate occasions spread over a period of up to 12 months. The staff interviewed (a total of just under 200 across the schools) were drawn from across the range of those who were believed to be in a position to comment on the nature and extent of changes in their school over the last five years[3] while a small number of interviews were also conducted with other key individuals (such as governors, advisers and support staff). Samples of Year 11 pupils were given group interviews. Some limited observation of lessons was also conducted in contrasting departments within the schools.

The emerging profiles of each institution were checked out on subsequent visits to the school and in discussion with senior groups of staff. A number of case studies of individual schools on different 'improvement trajectories' were also written up in greater detail at this point and helped to shape our strategies for identifying the main areas of change.

A second stage involved identifying (from the data assembled for each of the case studies of the 12 schools) some 20 dimensions along which changes were judged to have occurred. Working to a common framework, team members were asked to make a further judgement about the *amount* of change which had taken place in each of these various areas over the last five years (see Chapter 9). A third stage involved simple statistical analyses designed to establish whether any of these changes could be related to the schools' 'improvements in effectiveness' (see Chapter 10). At this latter stage we were particularly interested in any correspondence between the conclusions of the case studies and the statistical analyses.

Selecting schools for the case studies

We decided to start by developing case studies of individual institutions on different effectiveness/improvement trajectories. Such an approach gives pride of place to the specific circumstances of the individual case. The stories emerging from individual schools reveal mixtures of potential causes in which personalities, policies and practices become intertwined. It is part of the researcher's task, in telling each school's story, to try to understand their relative importance.

At the same time we were interested in moving beyond the confines of the specific case. During the writing-up stages, therefore, we adopted the idea of comparing schools with common starting-points and on similar improvement trajectories (see, for example, Wilcox *et al.* 1996). There is increasing interest among researchers and practitioners in establishing the extent to which local school contexts (so-called 'context-specificity') may determine the kinds of policies needed to move schools on (Teddlie and Stringfield 1993). Obviously a large number of such comparisons *could* be constructed. Eventually we focused on comparisons in relation to three particular groups of schools: schools which were initially less effective and improved only slowly over time; schools which were initially less effective but which began to improve rapidly; and schools which were initially effective and improved rapidly.

Our decision to focus on these three groups of schools was motivated by several concerns. We felt the policy interest at the current time was probably skewed towards the less effective schools. We needed, therefore, to compare and contrast pairs of schools on different improvement trajectories (see the accounts of Foxton and Burdland in Chapter 5 and Compton and Park in Chapter 6). At the same time, however, we wanted to understand rather more about the processes of rapid improvement from whatever starting-points schools might be at. This resulted in the pairing of two schools that were already effective when they started the improvement process (see the accounts of Rowland and Highdale in Chapter 8).

At this point we felt we were asking our readers to get close to no fewer than six of our 12 schools and we were reluctant to add detailed accounts of further cases. In reviewing the remaining six, therefore, we considered how far particular schools offered distinctively different accounts of the improvement process. We concluded that what had happened at Haystock did provide some alternative perspectives and consequently added it to the accounts in Chapter 5 of Foxton and Burdland. We also debated the position of Blackstone. In terms of its improvement trajectory it corresponded most closely to those of Compton and Park. However, while there were some similarities in the ways under-performance was tackled there were striking differences, notably in terms of the influence of personality. We eventually decided to give Blackstone space on its own (see Chapter 7). Finally, we were left with a decision about whether to describe what had gone on at Keystone, Aldley, Canonbury and Palmerton in fuller terms; given the space needed to do justice to them we felt we had already covered sufficient of the schools to meet our purposes.

Notes

1 Some background characteristics of the 12 schools are listed below:

Name of school	LEA	Background of school
Aldley	Hillshire	Secondary modern, creamed
Blackstone	Chesland	Urban comprehensive, some social disadvantage
Burdland	Hillshire	Urban comprehensive, considerable disadvantage
Canonbury	Chesland	Market town comprehensive
Compton	Hillshire	Market town comprehensive
Foxton	Chesland	Urban comprehensive, some disadvantage
Haystock	Midshire	Urban comprehensive, considerable disadvantage
Highdale	Hillshire	Market town comprehensive
Keystone	Chesland	Market town comprehensive
Palmerton	Midshire	Suburban comprehensive on edges of urban area
Park	Midshire	Urban comprehensive, considerable disadvantage
Rowland	Chesland	Market town comprehensive, some social advantage

2 The question of whether to keep the members of the research team assigned to each school in the dark about each school's performance was discussed at an early stage. The idea that they could be kept 'blind' throughout the study seemed implausible, not least because some of the schools being studied already had clear views of their performance which they communicated to the research team and which matched our own. We decided, however, not to make the school's performance category explicit until after some preliminary visits had been made so that early questioning of school members was not unduly coloured by the pursuit of answers to a specific concern.

3 The headteacher was invariably interviewed, regardless of how long he or she had been in the school. Interviews were also conducted, where appropriate, with chairs of governors, school secretaries and caretakers. Sometimes interviews were conducted with members of staff who had arrived at the school more recently. Such evidence as they provided was not ignored by members of the research team but was, for obvious reasons, excluded from some of the analyses of change.

5

STRUGGLING TO CHANGE

Schools can be all too easily stereotyped. Some are 'good', some are 'bad'. Some are 'moving', some are 'stuck'. It is sometimes difficult to discard the baggage of assumptions which go with these labels. We were quite surprised, therefore, how many changes had been initiated by the schools described in this chapter.

We look here at three schools, all initially less effective and, at best, only improving slowly over time.[1] The schools – Foxton, Haystock and Burdland – all cater for the 11–16 age range and draw upon catchment areas experiencing substantial disadvantage. However, because developments continued to a further stage at Haystock, at least in comparison with the other two schools, we have given rather more attention to its development in the latter part of the chapter.

Among the developments their heads and senior management teams (SMTs) mentioned were new approaches to planning, some reform of management structures and efforts to improve the schools' images in (and relationships with) their local communities. Further confirmation of some of these changes came from teachers. Very high proportions of the staff at Haystock, for example, thought that there had been 'substantial' changes over the last five years in the school's 'attitude and approach to planning', in the 'ways the school was run and organized' and in its 'ethos or culture'. Similarly high proportions of staff at Burdland noted 'substantial' changes in the school's attitude and approach to planning and the ways the school was run and organized; well over half reported changes in 'curriculum organization' at the same time. Teachers at Foxton were, at least in comparison to these other two schools, somewhat less likely to report initiatives, but even here well over half reported 'substantial' changes in the ways the school was run and organized and around half claimed to have seen similar levels of change in terms of the school's attitude and approach to planning and its curriculum organization.

There was also substantial agreement across heads and teachers that their schools faced problems – although perceptions of their seriousness varied. Pupils' achievements were known to be lagging behind those in other schools and all of them were subject to the problems of coping with (and trying to manage) falling rolls. Hardly any of the staff in any of the three schools thought there had been 'substantial' changes in the 'quality of teaching and learning'.

Reigns and honeymoons

When teachers retell what has been happening in their schools they almost invariably structure their accounts around the 'reigns' of the different headteachers under whom they have served. Their feelings about how well the school as a whole is doing are often bound up with their perceptions of the heads' performance. The arrival of a new head offers the prospect of change for those who seek it; even the more cynical seem prepared to suspend judgement during a new head's 'honeymoon'.

Roger Jones was the new incumbent at Haystock. He had been in post for about a year when we began visiting the school. Already an experienced headteacher, he recognized that one of his major tasks was 'to convince everyone that I am intending to see through a programme of school improvement'.

The previous head, John Atkinson, had been popular but had only been in post for just over two years before he moved on. Atkinson was widely perceived to be good with people, was seen to have lifted morale and to have raised the reputation of the school. A member of the SMT commented:

Atkinson was very high profile around the school and people liked that. He had a good way of talking to children, was very professional – like a polished after-dinner speaker.

A Year 11 pupil offered a view along similar lines:

Mr Atkinson raised the reputation of the school. He was the sort of person your mum fancied. He knew everyone's name. You could talk to him and have a joke.

Jones's style was very different from that of his predecessor. A member of the office staff spoke of the contrast:

Mr Atkinson was very affable, charismatic. He whipped us up into an enthusiasm which had been missing and people became willing to do things. He was the 'cosmetic' and we were carried away by his charisma but were not so aware of the practicalities. Roger put in the 'nitty-gritty'.

An inspector connected with the school confirmed the difference in style:

> Roger is up-front about planning. Planning under the previous head was very much presentational. Under Roger planning is more visionary and much better.

When Jim Peterson became head at Burdland he was already well known to his colleagues, having been in the school for the better part of 20 years, first as a head of department and then as a deputy. The previous head had been in post since the mid-1980s. He had had to cope with the school losing its sixth form and the threat of closure. By 1992 staff reported that morale had reached a low point. He had taken early retirement about 18 months before our first visit and shortly before an Ofsted inspection. Staff reported that he 'couldn't take the pressure' and that 'things had ground to a halt' some months before he finally left. The governors had appointed Peterson in an acting role, pending the appointment of a permanent replacement.

In the meantime, the school had to cope with the imminent inspection by Ofsted. With barely a couple of months to prepare, it faced considerable challenges. Given falling rolls, the school was already a potential candidate for closure and a 'poor' report could certainly have hastened the process. Peterson found himself 'plunged in at the deep end' and staff had steeled themselves for a 'damning' report.

As things turned out, while the inspectors found a good deal to criticize and recommended various changes, the school survived. In the aftermath (and after some delay, during which time the staff had written to the governors indicating that an internal appointment was a 'must'), the governors decided to appoint Peterson as head.

It is doubtful whether Peterson had the benefit of a 'honeymoon' period. Some staff had undoubtedly been impressed by the way he had led them through the inspection and felt that this gave him a good claim to the post; they were also prepared to give him the benefit of the doubt while he sought to introduce some changes.[2] For others, his main strength was that he already knew the school well and offered the prospect of much-needed stability. For still others, however, he was simply 'a known quantity', someone who understood and respected the status quo; some of this group were genuinely surprised when he started to show signs of wanting to change things.

The third head, Paul Black, had been in post considerably longer and since the time Foxton had first opened during the second half of the 1980s as a comprehensive school in purpose-built accommodation. Many staff could still recall the high hopes that had attended the school's opening and the comprehensive principles to which it was committed. As the head recalled:

> the culture of the school, the ethos of the school, is very much captured by the poster [we have on display] which says 'everyone matters'. It's a comprehensive school, we were the first purpose-built comprehensive school [in the LEA], we've always been a comprehensive school, I hope we always will be a comprehensive school. We believe every child matters, whatever their age, ability, their racial background and their social background. . . . Now I'm not saying that other schools don't have that but I think it pervades everything that we do.

Black's 'honeymoon' had lasted some while as staff committed themselves to making the new school work. Over time, however, and against the background of the increasing difficulties the school faced, a gap had begun to emerge between head and staff. Several features of the school's experiences over the intervening years could help to explain this. However, for some staff it was simply a matter of personality and a question of the head's 'remoteness'. One member of staff, who had been in the school since the beginning and who clearly still held him in high regard, none the less wanted him to 'let the staff know you're bleeding with them' about the difficulties the school was experiencing. Indeed, there were some signs that this advice had been taken on board; the head and SMT had launched a variety of initiatives designed to 'team-build'. But most of the optimism and goodwill that had attended the school's early years had, by the mid-1990s, drained away.

Ghosts and legacies

The urge to present a favourable picture is strong. While it is acceptable to confess to having some problems when a research team visits for the first time, few members of staff initially admit to their seriousness. We would argue, however, that one can only understand the present condition of these three schools if one takes account of their histories, in some cases going back considerably further than the five years we initially considered. Some of these 'past events' are like ghosts – they haunt the present. Beliefs about their existence constrain action. Others are more widely shared – whatever their objective status, they are seen as part of the common inheritance by members of staff which 'outsiders' must be helped to understand. Collectively, they represent a 'legacy' which has to be taken into account when changes are being contemplated.

By the end of the 1980s, Haystock's reputation was at a low ebb. The pupil intake had been declining in ability and its ethnic make-up had changed. Some teachers had had difficulty in adjusting to the changed intake and pupil discipline had deteriorated. As a lunch-time supervisor put it:

> When I first came to work here [in 1989] discipline was awful. There were gangs of pupils carrying knives. They couldn't get [lunch-time] supervisors to work here – they had to pay them double. They're still paid double but it's not so bad now.

Relationships between the headteacher and the remaining staff were deteriorating rapidly, exacerbated by what was seen as an authoritarian attitude on the part of the then head. As one class teacher reported:

> In 1990 there was an extremely closed door policy with underhand things going on. The head used to take people into the office and chastise them for speaking openly in staff meetings. As a result policies were not dealt with and there was a feeling of not working together.

These internal problems had, in turn, brought external repercussions. Ethnic communities in the school's catchment area had become worried that their needs were not being met by the school.

Old guards and dead men's shoes

The 'legacy' at Burdland included: the threat of closure; the period of weak and erratic leadership which had preceded Peterson's elevation to the headship; and falling pupil numbers owing to stiff competition for more able pupils in the locality. The SMT's energy was primarily devoted to trying to create the conditions for stability which were seen as a precondition for launching anything new. There had been some changes; staff were aware of them and, in many cases, supportive. But there were still problems. A head of department said:

> The morale of staff, since the cutbacks started, has gone down. People have had to double up their jobs to cope. . . . They are more wary of each other now. . . . We're still getting through this.

Indeed, reflecting on what was now needed in the school and the current balance of immediate priorities, one deputy remarked:

> When a school shrinks, the staff you are left with are the ones who aren't going anywhere. They block changes. These kinds of staff need the security that the place won't fall apart.

Furthermore, there was still a group of staff who were surprised by the extent to which the head was seeking changes to secure the school's future. They resented the position the school found itself in and the implications of these 'externally generated' problems for themselves. While they acknowledged that much of the change agenda was, indeed, 'externally generated', some of them were still resentful about Peterson's translation from colleague to head. As he pushed, they resisted. Getting frustrated by the limited pace of the reforms in the school, one teacher exclaimed:

> The old guard form a critical mass. They're a group of piss-takers who block change and the head is caught between them!

We judged the size of this group to be small in terms of the overall staff. However, having been in the school for many years, they were well established and influential. Any changes which were proposed had to take into account this 'culture of resistance'.

Foxton suffered from some similar problems. The head was aware of the need for changes but, after the first flurry of initiatives which had established the shape of the school when it was opening, internally generated improvements had become increasingly difficult to sustain. Many members of the school were simply unused to the challenge of developing their own agendas for change and resisted the SMT's efforts. As one head of department observed:

> I think, if you like, that developments occur from outside the school rather than within.

Falling rolls had restricted opportunities within the school for internal promotions. Around ten staff had taken early retirement in the last two or three years and there had been little or no 'new blood'. Crucially, there had been very few promotions indeed to middle or senior management positions, leaving a number of clearly talented teachers fairly disgruntled and cynical about the reward-to-effort ratios involved in securing change. In trying to explain some of the problems, one teacher remarked:

> There's been very little movement in this school for years. I mean in a shrinking school the chances of development are actually very little. I mean it's almost dead man's shoes, in fact that's where one or two people have got promotion here, literally. . . . Most of us have been in post for so long now and very few have been as fortunate as me as to have a refreshing change of direction down the line.

Other external factors had reinforced whatever sense of disenchantment already existed among staff and contributed to a tendency to blame factors beyond their control. Budget cuts, which the school had had to implement in successive years since the LEA's introduction of locally managed finances, featured prominently among the complaints. The head of science, for example, had some particularly strong views but was not untypical. Commenting on some of the ways in which cuts had eaten into the department's budget and affected the department's teaching, he complained:

Departments are expected to pay for examination tests, not national examinations but mock examinations and test papers, assessments and things like that. Also exercise paper, everything else. So it comes under stationery. Within science we've also got quite a severe health and safety bill. We then have capital equipment which needs repairing or replacing. Most of what we buy is either written on or poured down a sink or broken deliberately.... Our budget has gone down [by a quarter] since last year. We cannot manage on that.... For the last two to three years we have seen a quite dramatic and rapid decline in the equipment that's available. We are really down to rock bottom and below rock bottom.... We're wiping out our pupil open-ended investigatory type activities, which is the whole nature of science and we've opted out because we can't do it. Our pupils do not have textbooks, textbooks which match their ability.

Some teachers at the school had protested about the cuts to the LEA. However, others thought this had backfired and that the school was now 'branded'.

The head claimed to share much of his colleagues' frustration. The state of the school's accommodation, for example, had become a considerable worry and now represented a major impediment to progress:

there's not been enough investment in the accommodation here. ... Now that means that the buildings inside and outside, the grounds, everything connected with them has decayed and I haven't had the money to actually solve those problems.... I think that's a serious weakness of the school and all it needs is money to actually solve it. ... Another area which troubles me greatly is the fact that I've had to reduce staffing in recent years, partly because of general cutbacks in the LEA which have been awful over the last five years but also by the expansion of [other schools] which have taken children from this area and from my normal catchment.

Other members of staff saw the school's problems as being of longer standing. Seeking to explain the current sense of inertia among colleagues, one head of department commented:

It all goes back to the strikes of many years ago, ten years ago, when ... we had quite a militant staff and things like Saturday morning sports went, all the goodwill was removed. Things like residential trips went, after-school activities went. And I suppose as a staff we are not the youngest staff and we still have a lot of people who are quietly political.... Some of the things that have changed are a result of changing the house system to a year system. We no longer have house drama, sports day went last year and we no longer have house days.

Yet the disillusion felt by many staff did not generate the type of inter-staff conflict that seems to characterize many schools perceived as 'ineffective' or 'stuck' (Stoll and Myers 1997; Reynolds 1996). The group of staff who had dissociated themselves from active participation in school life amounted, in our judgement, to between a quarter and a third of the staff. What this group had created was a culture of 'retreat' rather than 'resistance'.[3] Indeed, the staffroom climate was still seen as good. One of the deputy heads commented:

> I think it is a very caring staff. I mean I've dealt with many different students and many different institutions ... [the staff] always make an effort to befriend supply teachers ... the common theme that comes through all of our visitors is that people take the time to talk ...

Part of Foxton's problem had become its own unwillingness to 'continue to fight' or 'take a stand'. Externalizing blame, limiting expectations and reducing their own efforts still further had become typical responses among its staff.

School contexts

We have so far avoided discussing the intakes to the schools and their catchment areas. This is mainly because the value-added analyses we conducted will have largely taken such factors into account. Staff in all three of these schools, however, took a rather different view. Each of the schools was usually seen by at least a sizeable minority of staff as the 'victim' of increased competition for pupils, a battle for survival in which their schools were not only not doing well but were treated unfairly. None of the schools, in fact, took anywhere near the full range of pupils from its immediate catchment area.

Foxton was supposed to have a 'balanced' catchment area; it included housing for both working- and middle-class families. Initially the purpose-built accommodation had seemed an added attraction. Over the years since its opening, however, it had found itself losing the more advantaged pupils to other schools. A head of department commented on some of the difficulties the school had experienced in the following terms:

> Home background is different now, it is not as good as it used to be because of the area they come from and ability levels. You know the VRQs [Verbal Reasoning scores] are very low and we don't get many high ones at all; and I personally think that when we talk about the type of child that we get at this school we could actually be going down a line of really doing something for those sorts of

pupils as well as the more academic, which is what we are trying to do because we've setted a more able group at the moment.

Burdland served a very much more disadvantaged catchment than Foxton, composed almost exclusively of areas devoted to council housing (the more traditional, semi-detached kind) and with a relatively high proportion of pupils on free school meals. It was the only secondary school in its 'community'. A member of the SMT, however, remarked on the extent to which it too had lost its 'top end'. More 'ambitious' parents frequently tried to get their children into schools some distance beyond the immediate boundaries of the locality; with spare capacity available in these institutions, they usually succeeded.

The pupil intake to Haystock did not reflect its immediate surroundings either. Situated in a middle-class area several miles from the city centre, the school had changed dramatically during the late 1980s when catchment areas had been redrawn. It now drew a mere 20 per cent of its intake from the area. The remaining 80 per cent came from inner-city areas and a high proportion were on free school meals. In terms of ethnic composition, about half the pupils were white, a substantial minority were Asian and around one-tenth were Afro-Caribbean. Already a small school in terms of pupil numbers and branded as 'one of the worst schools in the city' in the late 1980s, there was apparently some discussion around this time as to whether it too should be closed.

Within a value-added framework for analysing schools' performances the 'disadvantaged' natures of the schools' catchment areas should not, of course, explain their levels of effectiveness, or should do so only marginally. But, in fact, the problems associated with social disadvantage and 'creamed' intakes clearly figured prominently in the legacy with which each school had to deal. Such concerns also formed part of the backdrop against which efforts to improve had to be formulated. A good deal of the energy (and especially that of the senior management) that might otherwise have been devoted to developing and sustaining change efforts *within* the schools was actually spent shoring up relationships with local communities to make sure the school survived.

Coming to terms with the need for change

Foxton was Paul Black's creation. He had developed a vision for the school as a potentially thriving 'comprehensive', appointed its staff and formulated its policies. In the early 1990s he found himself obliged to reconsider some of his approaches and long-held beliefs. Some of the pressures on him for change were internally generated, others reflected external factors as the school found itself competing for pupils in the market-place.

Responding to staff criticism, he had introduced a new approach to development planning within the school. The role of development planning was given a much more central place in the school's approach. In the process, Black relinquished his role as sole writer and formulator of the plan. At the same time he made deliberate efforts to involve more staff in the policy-making process. The enhanced use of working parties bypassed the usual organizational structure – changes to school policies were increasingly informed by their deliberations. These changes were also accompanied by some reforms to the SMT; the intention of these was to make the SMT larger, more inclusive and more 'lateral' in organization.

There was one other major reform to the school's organization. Originally built around a house system for pastoral care, the school switched over to a year system. While this change had gone through, however, without too much resistance, there was a feeling that heads of year were finding it difficult to take a leading role in co-ordinating the academic work of their pupils.

Finally, some effort had been made to improve the school's image in the local community. A press publicity officer had been appointed; interestingly, this person was given responsibility for aspects of the school's physical appearance as well.

These organizational changes had clearly had effects, albeit rather limited ones.[4] Some staff certainly felt more involved than previously in formulating the directions the school was taking. However, in the main, the changes were experienced by staff as initiatives of the SMT's making; they had become pretty skilled at marginalizing them.

Developing a strategy for survival

Jim Peterson's introduction to the headship at Burdland had been a 'baptism of fire' which he had survived. His 'street cred' among some of the staff had undoubtedly risen as a result. Having been in the school a long time he felt he had a keen sense of what needed to be done, although the inspectors' recommendations had added considerably to his agenda.

The main challenge, as he saw it, was to persuade his erstwhile colleagues that they needed to change. Within a relatively short period a number of modest initiatives had been launched across the school. Peterson, however, seems to have concentrated his initial energies in just four areas.

The first related to the SMT's management style. His predecessor had been perceived as remote and aloof. Peterson was aware that he had been part of the previous regime and therefore had to make strenuous efforts to establish that things were going to be different. At the same time, his analysis told him that, along with a change in the SMT's management style, he needed to launch a more consensual and participative approach to planning, which he had already begun to do.

The community's attitude towards the school was crucial to its survival. With a falling roll, the school could ill afford to lose *any* pupils to neighbouring schools. Indeed, in the short term and in order to make ends meet, it showed some willingness to take on pupils whom other secondary schools in the area had discarded, whatever the problems they might bring with them. Demographic trends within the community were unlikely to help. To stay at its present size and with a similar complement of staff, the school needed to recruit virtually *all* the pupils in its catchment area and a few more besides.

Peterson made winning back the community's confidence and respect a particular priority. This was, of course, going to be both demanding of his energies and time-consuming – a lot of lost ground needed to be recovered. The messages he took to parents' evenings at local primary schools were succinct. The school was not going to close, it had a future, the inspectors had found 'much to praise' and so on. At the same time he made strenuous efforts to bring the community back into the school. He was available, he stressed, to see parents; they could come straight to the top if they wanted; it was 'their school' and it needed their support.

Allied to these efforts (and intended to reinforce them), he had set about improving the school's physical appearance. The school's foyer had recently been refurbished, there were signs of redecoration in other parts of the school and some new carpets had been laid. More changes were being planned.

His fourth strategy was to seek external support. Burdland had been a source of concern to its LEA advisory service for some time. Peterson realized that the advisers were keen to help and began to take steps to involve them. As a result, advisers had started to visit the school to encourage and support teachers as they reviewed what changes they needed to initiate. Staff had been cautious at the beginning and were still rather tentative but were, Peterson felt, opening up a little.

There were several signs therefore that, as one adviser put it, the 'seeds of change' were being planted. There was still much to work on and the school faced a 'long haul', but there was cautious optimism that it had 'turned the corner and had a future'. There were, however, some who thought that the problems outweighed the progress. A head of department complained that:

The SMT won't grasp some of the problems. . . . Staff won't show a united front. There are now policies in place but they aren't being monitored and pupils aren't necessarily being followed up.

Unfortunately, around this time something happened at the school which was beyond the school's control but affected everyone. The school that was 'going to close' now had another 'label' to cope with.[5] Peterson remained outwardly optimistic, but the challenges were formidable.

The long haul back from the brink

Those who were there at the time say that 1990 was the crunch year for Haystock. The catchment area had been changed; the pupil intake was very different; and there were tensions with the ethnic communities who now formed a considerable proportion of the school's clientele. Furthermore, relations were said to be poor between the SMT and the remainder of the staff. To compound the problems the school was facing, the head (who had been in post throughout the previous decade) was away with increasing frequency due to ill health. The school struggled on for another year with a deputy covering for the head. By the end of the year, however, both the head and this deputy had retired and the other deputy, Peter Butler, was appointed as acting head.

Butler's first priority was to stop the downward spiral of staff morale. He focused on making the new SMT more open to staff – an intention which was symbolized by the early removal of the 'traffic lights' outside the head's office. More significantly, he was concerned to make more information available to staff about the school's priorities and to involve them directly in the planning processes.

When the permanent position was advertised, Butler applied but was not successful.[6] John Atkinson took up the headship in mid-1992. He recruited a new deputy and set about what he saw as the main task – restoring the community's confidence in the school. The challenge was not easy. In 1993, for example, the school had its worst ever exam results.[7] None the less, as the school secretary told us:

John could charm the birds off the trees and he did much to convince parents not to write the school off.

Atkinson's period as head, however, was relatively brief. He stayed until the end of 1994, when he left for another headship in a larger institution. Among a small staff personalities were felt to matter; many staff undoubtedly felt let down. Roger Jones, already an experienced head, took over.

To summarize, then, over a five-year period the small staff of the school had been served by no fewer than four headteachers (including the acting head) and an SMT which had changed, both in terms of its membership and the roles it assumed. Some teachers found the lack of continuity in leadership was itself a problem.

The challenges for improvement

When Butler took over as acting head he faced three clear challenges: to improve relationships within the school; to improve relationships between the school and its communities; and to arrest the decline in achievement in general and examination results in particular. Butler's appointment, albeit a temporary one, undoubtedly initiated a more open style of management which Atkinson and Jones successively extended. Staff morale began to improve although it was still said, several years later, to be potentially 'volatile'.

Before 1990 planning had been 'done on the hoof'. Under Butler a start was made on using the management plan *inter alia* as a vehicle for rather more staff involvement. The plan covering the period 1990–92 had been elaborate but not used. In establishing a new plan for 1992–95, Butler was concerned to identify genuine priorities and to get departments to produce their own plans. This plan had begun to be implemented when Atkinson arrived and was essentially maintained over the following three years.

Under Jones's leadership planning (and staff involvement in planning) continued to develop. The 1995–98 plan was made widely available by its inclusion in the staff handbook. It contained targets and offered structured deadlines. This was just one sign of the success of the strategy initiated by Butler to encourage more staff involvement. Governors also began to receive more detailed and informative documentation. Staff generally felt they were now consulted more often and were perhaps, in the view of at least one teacher, even in 'danger of being 'over-consulted'. Issues related to discipline and difficult relationships with some of the ethnic groups in the school were undoubtedly central to Haystock's poor reputation at the time Butler took over. The development of an 'equal opportunities' policy became an early priority for him. Eventually, after some stormy meetings, he was able to convince parents that their complaints about racial issues would be taken seriously. Staff assigned to the school (under Section 11 funding for community relations) played a key role in mediating relationships between the school and its community at this time and there were several signs that these policies had been working. An Asian pupil, for example, told us:

> I feel comfortable here because there are lots of people from my own community – and others.

Atkinson continued to work on the school's reputation during his period of office, and this was one of Jones's priorities when he took over. In 1995 a newsletter was introduced as one way of emphasizing the importance of maintaining parental and community support. More efforts were put into liaison with primary schools, and again there were signs that the changes were taking hold.[8] Reputations, however, are always likely to be vulnerable for a school like Haystock with a media 'reputation' in the not-too-distant past. More recently, a pupil brandishing a toy gun in the school had ended up in the local press as 'a stabbing'.

Butler's initial influence on the discipline front was also evident. He had introduced a code of conduct. Atkinson had kept up the impetus, and his influence was widely acknowledged. One teacher told us:

> [Atkinson] seemed extremely caring and open to children and gave them a sense of being listened to and being important. Strong messages were given by him in assemblies – there was great sensitivity in his approach.

Under Jones the code of conduct was revamped by a working party. It included a detailed prescription of classroom expectations and was again recognized to have had some influence although, as one member of the SMT observed, it now 'needed another boost'. A pupil told us that:

> The teachers are now more strict, so there is not so much messing about as there used to be. This is better. We noticed the improvement.

To combat discipline problems during break-times Jones extended the lunch-time clubs Atkinson had set up. A school council was established, which had contributed to the construction of the revamped code of conduct, and a reward system (offering pupils commendations and certificates) had been introduced. Both initiatives seem to have helped. However, a minority of staff (and some pupils) thought the current regime was less keen on maintaining discipline than the previous one. Such perceptions were linked in part to Jones's unwillingness to exclude pupils (as the previous head had done) and his greater willingness to take on pupils who had been excluded from other schools.

Arresting the decline in achievement

By the time of Jones's arrival, Haystock had managed to reclaim at least part of its reputation. He quickly realized, however, that little had happened in relation to the third of the three challenges the school had been set – pupils' achievements needed to improve considerably.[9]

Butler had started work in two departments in the school (science and maths) where pupils appeared to be under-performing at GCSE, bringing in LEA advisory staff to help. The momentum had slackened, however, under Atkinson, although he had supported the efforts of a Section 11 team within the school. They had set up a mentoring scheme for black pupils, encouraged them to become involved in reading partnerships and a lunch-time reading club; introduced a bank of resources on 'black perspectives' which parents could use when their children were not given homeworks; and were the prime movers behind a pupil planner which allowed parents to see a record of the homework their children had been set. After-school classes had also been introduced in 1994 for Year 11 pupils who wanted them. Jones noted these initiatives but felt that more needed to be done. In particular, he was keen to build up a focus on teaching and learning within the classroom.

Value-added data on pupils' performance (available from the LEA) were brought to teachers' attention and used to help convince them of pupils' potential. Building on this, Jones carried out an exercise using a structured interview schedule in which all heads of department were individually questioned about their examination results. Several expressed some shock about what the data revealed. The growing recognition that the school was, indeed, under-performing provided the basis for the 1995–98 development plan which was built around the theme of 'raising achievement'. There were seven priorities: the quality of teaching; equal opportunities; curriculum; assessment; behaviour management; home and school community; and attendance.

This new-found commitment to improve pupils' achievements was apparent among many of the staff we interviewed. A member of the SMT explained:

We are about achievement – if you have kids who don't know why they are here you have to do something with them. Children now realize they are here to achieve. On the other hand, on the negative side, some kids are not hard-working and the moment you put pressure on them you can have problems – the culture of working hard has not reached them yet.

It was proving difficult, however, to provide pupils with much extra support. The mentoring scheme set up in 1994 was not 'officially' running during 1995 because of staffing difficulties; and a similar fate befell the after-school classes provided for Year 11 pupils in the following year.

The emphasis on teaching and learning

Teaching at Haystock was not easy. Indeed, many staff felt that there had been an increase in the extent of 'challenging' pupil behaviour in recent years which had consequences for what could be taught in the classroom. A languages teacher told us:

A different kind of teaching is necessary [at this school] – you have to plan a lot more carefully and ensure that the lesson content is clearly relevant to the children. If you move them on too quickly you soon lose them. Pupils come into lessons sometimes not wanting to work, and if you make them work they can be difficult.

Shortly after taking up his post Jones decided to launch his most ambitious initiative. He realized that the school had little or no tradition of discussing teaching and learning and felt this was crucial to its subsequent development. The LEA inspector attached to the school encouraged him in this belief and offered the support Jones felt he needed:

> He's been a crucial player in the school's attempt to raise achievement. . . . He is intellectual and has a challenging approach. If I had a problem I could phone him at home at any time.

During his first two terms, therefore, he interviewed every member of staff about their professional aspirations and their views of the school. He followed this up the following term with a programme of classroom observation which resulted in his seeing the teaching of every member of staff.

This was potentially a very high-risk strategy; the details required a good deal of negotiation with the staff. A sophisticated observation schedule was, however, constructed and used; time was made available to discuss the lessons observed with the staff members concerned; and the confidentiality of the completed schedules was respected. Staff reactions to the exercise were generally favourable. One head of department said:

> The head [has been] doing classroom observation. He has explained this very well and given everyone a pro forma and called a meeting for anyone with doubts. The observation schedule works and you get feedback very quickly and the completed pro forma. It can be good to see the written feedback. You say to yourself: did I really do that?

Work continued on this front during the following year with a further series of individual discussions with all teaching and support staff. Arising out of this exercise came some consideration of the factors which led to effective and ineffective lessons. These results were circulated to staff, and departments were encouraged to refine the list of factors further. At the same time new staff appointed to the school were brought into the programme.

Most of this work was initially with individuals. Towards the end of Jones's first year as head, a professional development group was started to explore the theme 'the quality of learning'. The group was voluntary, informal and met at lunch-time – it was hoped that one outcome would be that teachers would agree to observe each other teaching. At the same time Jones attempted to widen the circle of people teachers could potentially learn from. He actively sought involvement with LEA and higher education partners and organized visits to other 'comparable' schools to break down some of the school's insularity.

Jones was clearly making some progress in terms of school-wide strategies. However, there were also problems. Two or three of the major subject departments had weak leadership and difficult relationships. Some of the heads of department had been in post for a number of years and were doubtful about some of the changes that had been introduced. They continued to lament the levels of discipline, complained about the paperwork and deadlines and worried about their own positions. Collectively they represented a critical mass, united not so much in opposition as in scepticism.

Such difficulties were exacerbated by staff absences due to stress and illness. As a result the school had had to rely heavily on supply teachers. These were often the subject of critical comment by pupils:

> Some teachers get too stressed. They have nervous breakdowns. Then we have a lot of supply teachers. This is a problem because they can't control the classes.

Not only did continuity suffer in such circumstances but also the actual quality of what got taught:

> There are too many supply teachers. They just work from textbooks. They don't actually teach you or help you.

The school's heavy reliance on supply cover also brought other problems:

> A lot of staff are off ill . . . so we can't get our coursework in because there is no expert help. Supply teachers come and go so we don't know where we are. We will not get the grades we deserve because we don't have a teacher.

There were, none the less, various signs by the end of 1996 that the school had improved and could be cautiously optimistic. Relationships with the ethnic communities had been re-established since the tensions six years previously; John Atkinson's unexpected and early departure had largely been worked through; the school's physical accommodation had been much enhanced; clear structures for the school's planning and organization were in place; and there had even been small improvements in exam results since the nadir of 1993. Furthermore, the school had been exposed in 1996 to the full glare of an Ofsted inspection and survived. The inspectors had concluded that 'Haystock (was) developing well under the good leadership of a recently-appointed headteacher'.

How robust the school's 'improvement culture' had actually become was shortly to receive a considerably more stringent test. Half-way through his third year in the school, Jones told staff that he would be leaving at the end of the summer term for the headship of a larger school in another city. As he left, the longer-serving staff at Haystock prepared themselves for their fifth headteacher in seven years.

Concluding comments

Although the schools had different origins and histories, all three had found themselves in similar predicaments during the five years that our study considered. All had experienced significant changes in the composition of their catchment areas, problems with local communities, difficulties in managing falling pupil numbers, budget restrictions and the threat of closure. In addition, at some point during this same period, they had been characterized by low staff morale, general developmental apathy and low levels of pupil performance.

Improvement from such a baseline represented a formidable challenge. The total quantum of staff energy for change was, of course, finite and much of it was consumed in attempting to keep the schools functioning on a day-to-day basis as viable institutions. Much of whatever energy was available for change had to be focused within the schools. Of comparable importance, however, was the restoration and maintenance of support and regard from their communities and, in particular, their parent bodies.

The pattern of internal reforms undertaken varied somewhat in detail from school to school, reflecting the needs of their specific contexts. Nevertheless, some similarities in the developmental priorities they chose to adopt are apparent. Attention was given to matters relating to: the structure and style of the senior management; the need to make planning more systematic and participative; the restructuring, to some degree, of middle management roles; and the active marketing of the school. These initiatives can generally be understood as a 'loosely coupled' change strategy of which the most explicit example was at Haystock.

What can be seen in each of these schools resulted from initiating and implementing a number of specific changes, implicitly regarded as constitutive of school improvement. In only one of the three cases (Haystock), however, does one see the beginnings of an attempt to influence classroom teaching and learning directly. Taking the changes over the whole five-year period at Haystock, a possible developmental model may be discerned in which an emphasis on teaching and learning emerges at a later stage than initiatives relating to the community and the school's organization, management and ethos. An important question for the present study is whether this order is invariant. Can teaching and learning initiatives emerge successfully earlier on?

Notes

1 These schools had at best improved slowly in terms of their effectiveness over the last five years in terms of the framework outlined in Figure 4.2. None of the schools in this category had been judged (or was likely to be judged) by Ofsted

as 'failing', although inspectors could be expected to identify some 'serious concerns' in relation to each.

2 Although the school's staff had been temporarily lifted by the inspection, the threats it potentially represented to the school's existence persisted. Several members of staff interviewed by the research team had to be persuaded that members of the research team were not some kind of 'advance guard' for a further inspection before they would allow themselves to be interviewed.

3 What we termed 'sources of resistance' took different forms in different schools but were present, to a greater or lesser extent, in half the schools we studied. In Burdland and Foxton we judged the group of 'resisters' to be small but none the less influential, while in Haystock there were also still some vestiges.

4 During the latter stages of the research the team made judgements about the amounts of change which had occurred in each of the 12 schools. Overall, and in comparison with nearly all the other schools, Foxton was rated across most of the dimensions as experiencing 'little or no change'; only in the area of management structures did the team conclude that there had been 'a lot of change'.

5 To reveal what actually happened would substantially compromise the school's identity. Suffice it to say that whatever impetus the school had built up to change around this time had to be put largely on hold. Our commitment to fieldwork was ending around this time and we felt it was inappropriate to keep up more than minimal contact thereafter. At the time of writing the school had recovered and was generally felt to have a somewhat more secure future.

6 Butler retired from his position as deputy two years later but stayed on subsequently as a part-time classroom teacher.

7 This was, of course, one of the first years in which the full effects of the changes to the catchment area in the late 1980s would have been experienced.

8 Surveys which the school and Ofsted carried out confirmed that community perceptions of the school were generally favourable.

9 The story from this point onwards is of interest because it reveals the new head's analysis about what had been missing at Haystock and what it now needed to do. Given the timing of the fieldwork, however, the actual impact of these activities on subsequent cohorts of pupils was beyond the scope of this project.

6

GETTING INTO THE PACK

This chapter is about two ordinary schools. Until recently neither would have been deemed of interest to the wider world. Neither was engaged in especially innovative curriculum strategies and neither was at the cutting edge of school improvement. None the less, we would argue that what has been going on at these two schools merits attention.

Five years ago both schools were identified by value-added analyses as 'less effective'; since that time both have improved 'rapidly'. Neither can, as yet, claim to be of more than average effectiveness and, in one case, even this position is not yet fully established. Within the frameworks of the present study, however, they assume a wider importance because each pursued similar strategies to 'get back into the pack'.

The evidence for change and improvement

Park School is a small comprehensive. It opened in the late 1970s and occupies an attractive site on the outskirts of a large urban area. With some 40 per cent of its pupils on free school meals, however, it has been constantly dealing with the problems of social disadvantage. Although few of its pupils have been formally statemented as having special educational needs, a much larger number have been identified as having learning and other difficulties. If one uses the national average as a criterion for judging performance, then current standards fall well below it. The national average is not, however, an appropriate statistic against which to judge Park's performance. By the mid-1990s it had tackled its relative under-performance and was beginning to perform on a par with schools with comparable intakes.

There were several other signs that the school had turned the corner. The most obvious of these was that many staff not only felt there had been changes but were prepared, when challenged, to articulate reasons why and how such changes had occurred. When asked to consider achievement more generally (and not just as measured by exam performance) and to compare the school's position now with that which had prevailed five years previously, some 60 per cent rated the changes as amounting to a 'substantial' improvement. Other dimensions on which the majority of staff were equally confident that 'improvement' had taken place included the organization of the school, its ethos, its arrangements for planning, and its curriculum organization and delivery.

Academic expectations at Compton, a large comprehensive which took almost the full ability range, were considerably higher. In its case the national average seems a much more relevant figure for judging performance. Serving a small market town and its surrounding villages, one's immediate impression is of a relatively advantaged (although not especially prosperous) catchment area. The take-up of free school meals, at under 10 per cent, suggests that poverty was not a major factor.

Compton's claim to have 'improved' does not necessarily strike one immediately from the 'raw' statistics. Its performance over the last five years has usually been within striking distance of national averages. But there was no apparent surge, for example, in the statistics that might alert one to an improving situation. It emerged as a school which was improving in its effectiveness because, over each of the last five years, it had been securing a little more from a pupil population whose average performance at intake had been declining a little. A few years ago it was under-performing. Since then it had not only moved safely into the pack but even showed some tentative signs of pulling ahead. Without a sophisticated value-added analysis, however, the school would not have come to anyone's attention.

Staff at Compton were just as confident that improvements in achievement (broadly construed) had occurred as those at Park. Again, about 60 per cent rated them as 'substantial'. In one particular respect, however, they differed markedly from their counterparts at Park. Just under half the Park staff thought changes in the 'quality of teaching and learning' had been 'substantial'. By contrast only just over one in ten of Compton's staff thought the same.

Some starting-points

Change is a continuous process that cannot be neatly defined as having started at a particular time. None the less, teachers at Park were prepared to identify a specific point at which the most recent round of changes had begun. There was widespread agreement about this. The appointment, in the early 1990s, of Valerie Jameson as headteacher had ushered in a period which was recognizably different from previous times.

Mrs Jameson's ability to revitalize a declining school was attested by all. She was described as 'an outstanding headteacher' who had 'a clear vision' and an 'open style of management'. She was perceived as 'flexible without being fuzzy' and 'very supportive of staff'. She was, as one teacher put it, 'the pivot around whom everything revolved'.

From shortly after her arrival Mrs Jameson had been able to introduce a broadly coherent approach to change because many of the staff in post already recognized that the school had been stagnating and was in need of major improvement. Fears of possible closure lurked in the background, and the imminence of an Ofsted inspection also helped to concentrate minds. She, for her part, recognized that she had to assume the 'driving seat' from the beginning to get things going. As she put it:

> The majority of people are only too willing to be led. This is a particular problem with a slightly ageing staff – there is nothing in it for them.

Teachers agreed with her analysis. Once things were under way, however, she felt able to pull back, to some extent, and leave matters to others.

Staff at Compton had more difficulty in identifying a specific point in time for the change process. The present headteacher, Tom Randall, had been in post since the early 1970s and so there was no obvious time at which one head had stepped down and another taken over. Those whose experience stretched back that far remarked that the present head had inherited a difficult situation. Founded in the mid-1960s from an amalgamation of local grammar and secondary modern schools, the school's early years had been marked by internal turmoil and strained relationships with the local community. Randall was remembered for having established the school on a firmer basis.

During the early 1990s a process of change had begun which had acquired its own momentum but also taken on extra urgency in the context of various external initiatives. The LEA had been in the vanguard of those who were concerned to help schools improve their pupils' performances, and the publication of league tables gave this concern additional urgency. More recently an Ofsted inspection had concentrated views still further. While such events had undoubtedly added to the impetus for change, however, the change process was widely identified as having started *just before* 1990.

There was no comparable catalyst at Compton to mirror the arrival of Mrs Jameson at Park. The nearest one came to this was in the frequency with which Bob Drake's name was mentioned. Drake had been in the school almost as long as Randall, the headteacher who had appointed him as a 'rookie'. He had been promoted successively from classroom teacher to year leader to senior teacher. Finally, and most recently, recognizing

Drake's talents and influence, Randall had promoted him to the SMT as an assistant head. He was to be, as Randall put it, 'the standards man'. When staff discussed the various initiatives the school had taken, they found it hard to date the start of the process precisely. Drake's influence was, however, often mentioned. In the words of one long-serving teacher:

He has done a lot in a short space of time [and] has moved the school in the right direction.

Another said:

It's all down to Mr Drake.

A third remarked that:

You need people to drive policies forward. In this school that person is Bob Drake.

Between them the two schools had mounted more than a dozen initiatives. For the purposes of presentation we have grouped these loosely under three broad headings. These describe the activities the schools initiated to: focus on achievement; to develop ethos; and to address their public images.

The focus on achievement

Both schools were in LEAs which had encouraged the systematic use of data on examination results to monitor both schools' and departments' performance at least a year or two before league tables were published nationally. Such activities had helped to raise teachers' expectations of pupils' capabilities and alerted them to the possible need for action. These developments had got rather further at Compton than at Park, where more detailed scrutiny of the available evidence began to be taken seriously around the time of Mrs Jameson's arrival. As public dissemination of its results loomed, however, such activities acquired a fresh urgency at Compton. The SMT began to look at departments' results more closely. Value-added analyses had already identified some more general issues but, as the head put it:

league tables pricked us into activity. Previously there was little comparison. Most departments assumed the intake was bottom-heavy but in fact it was not much different from other schools. Staff cannot use this as an excuse any more once other schools with similar kids do better. So now we question how we can do things better, too.

Staff at Park had been aware of issues about the school's performance before Mrs Jameson's arrival but not a great deal had been done about them.

The analyses their LEAs had facilitated allowed the SMTs in both schools to place their interactions with departments on a more informed basis and, in time, led to the more formal discussion of actual targets. As Compton's head put it:

> We have become much more sharply focused over the last few years – previously we didn't tackle standards with departments. Now we are pulling together better as a staff.

More recently, and building in part on their LEAs' analyses, both schools had identified the under-achievement of boys as a priority.

The two SMTs now placed a lot more emphasis on monitoring aspects of departments' performance than previously. Both teams were aware of which departments had changed for the better over the period, particularly in terms of exam results, as well as those which had changed little. How to turn around less effective departments had become a constant preoccupation, especially at Park. The appointment of new heads of department, when the opportunity arose, was seen as the best hope for change. Events did not always work out this way, however. One departmental head at Park had been absent due to sickness for a long time. This, and a succession of supply teachers, had led to problems of discipline. A new head of department had been appointed but, within a year, had offered his resignation.

Both schools began to grow more 'streetwise' in their choice of examination boards. Departmental heads were encouraged to consider the extent to which specific boards met their curricular objectives and to choose boards, at least partly, on the basis of those likely to give the best grades. Such reviews did not, however, necessarily result in any changes. In the maths department at Compton the board was changed because it was thought that an A grade was easier to secure from another examining group. In addition, the new board required less coursework which meant there was more time to teach the syllabus. Unfortunately, the syllabus of the old board was seen as providing a better preparation for A level. Since many pupils at the school stayed on into the sixth form, potentially enhanced performance at GCSE had to be weighed against the later consequences.

Monitoring pupil achievement and mentoring pupils featured prominently in both schools. Park had developed a comprehensive system of monitoring in which pupils in each year group were assessed every eight weeks. A special form was completed on pupils within each department on their progress and effort. Results were collated and letters of 'praise' sent to parents where merited. This system was backed up by a mentoring process which had been expanding to cover increasingly large numbers of pupils. This more recent development had been extended in the last two years to all Year 11 pupils. Initially each member of the SMT had had a number of mentees drawn from those pupils considered to be borderline in reaching the crucial level of five GCSE passes at grades A–C. The head, however, had had some doubts. She felt that focusing on this specific group 'gave the wrong message' and so the scheme had subsequently been extended to all Year 11 pupils. Every member of staff had therefore been given five mentees. The aim was to meet at least once each half term to help pupils with their general preparation for GCSE.

A monitoring/mentoring system was also employed at Compton although the commitment to it was somewhat less extensive than at Park. In its final stages (during the last half term of Year 11 before the exams) it involved all the SMT and heads of year as mentors of pupils in the 'borderline five A–C grades' category as well as 'under-achieving able pupils'. Most pupils seem to have found some aspect of mentoring helpful and, in some cases, it appears to have had a significant effect. A Year 12 pupil at Compton told us:

> I had Mr Kirk. If I had kept going the way I was, I would have got all Ds. He pushed me, and it worked. I got Cs. He helped me to express what the teachers were telling me. Expressing myself has always been my problem.

Teachers in the two schools were not only involved in more monitoring and mentoring activities, but also did more teaching. Both sought to boost the exam performance of Year 11 pupils by the provision of extra classes after school. One of these pupils at Park said:

> A good thing in this school is that if you don't understand, there are revision lessons after school and extra classes during the Easter holiday.

Park had even extended provision to include a lunch-time study class. While going along with such developments, the Compton head wondered, however, how far things could be pushed in this direction and expressed some anxieties:

> If teachers give extra teaching time and then the pupils do better than such pupils previously did, the success of the pupils is not because the teachers are now better teachers but because the pupils get more teaching time. But if teachers work that hard over and above contractual requirements, most cannot sustain it. And it is also dependent on the goodwill of the teachers. I question whether it is wise to depend on a strategy of overworking teachers in order to improve results.

Building expectations

Raising levels of academic achievement must ultimately be related to the quality of the classroom experience encountered by pupils throughout their time in school. A key development here was the introduction of codes of classroom conduct. Of course, both schools had, in the past, had general statements about pupil discipline, but the formalization of such a code was seen as a distinctive step on the road to change. Park's code stated that 'all pupils have a right to learn and all teachers have a right to teach'. The code was prominently displayed in classrooms and was generally thought to have been useful. A head of department at Park described it in the following terms:

> The code is a quick device, a common language for dealing with minor offences with key words like 'off task' – it provides a quick reminder without interrupting everyone in the class . . . [also] pupils now bring to lessons everything they need which was a problem in the past.

Like many other schools, both had introduced pupil planners. This was seen as an aid in systematizing pupils' approaches to learning. The Park version of the planner (apart from space for recording details of lessons, homework set and 'merit stickers' received) included a termly review sheet for completion by the pupil in conjunction with each subject teacher. This allowed a rating to be made of homework, effort and so on, as well as the setting of specific targets for the pupil. In addition, the Key Stage 4 planner included an outline strategy for revision. Planners were generally regarded as useful, although Year 11 pupils reported some decline in the frequency with which entries were checked by tutors.

Resources for learning

Several changes to the learning environment were identified. The library/ resource areas of both schools had been significantly upgraded. In Compton a major remodelling and extension of the library had occurred involving active collaboration with the local library service. Pupils in both schools also identified the growth in computers and their use in classes as a beneficial change. Park pupils were particularly enthusiastic:

> There are more computers now. They are used all the time, in most subjects. We feel competent to use them. We have got a new network and have been taught how to use it.

Compton teachers acknowledged the contribution made by their learning support department and identified some of the changes which had taken place in recent years. In 1992 it had been reconstituted to bring it in line with the LEA's change to a policy of integration. The department was now funded as a designated centre, partly by the LEA and partly by the school. Learning support staff provided both withdrawal and in-class support. Integration meant that much more differentiated work was possible – the department was able to prepare extra worksheets for both less and more able pupils. Park, however, lacked a comparably funded department and the headteacher was concerned that pupils with special educational needs were being integrated without support at a time when the school was receiving more emotionally disturbed children. At Compton concerns about reading standards had begun to lead to initiatives in the teaching of reading to Year 7 pupils. Although too late to influence the period with which we were chiefly concerned, it is of interest that by early 1996 this had become a whole-school reading initiative.

As part of their comprehensive traditions the schools had both adopted mixed-ability teaching. More recently, there had been a move towards setting by ability. In both the timing had been left to departments. Setting had been a long-established practice at Compton but a more recent innovation at Park. Pupils were generally in agreement that setting was the preferred mode for organizing learning.

Both schools 'rediscovered' access to textbooks for individual pupils. This was generally seen as an important prerequisite for pupils' learning. Pupils particularly valued the opportunity of having their own textbook which they could take home (as was exceptionally the case in the science department at Compton). Park pupils in the top modern languages set of Year 11 had even purchased their own copies of the textbook.

Interestingly, staff development had followed on from the focus on achievement rather than preceding it. Both schools had recently focused on the teaching and learning process through in-house professional development activities. At Compton these had led to a policy of 'effective learning'. Park's staff were increasingly encouraged to attend external courses. The SMT here was strongly committed to staff development, reflecting the school's recent accreditation as an 'Investors in People' organization. As part of this commitment it was members of the SMT who provided cover for teachers away on staff development.

Summary

Teachers in both schools recognized that a more explicit 'focus on achievement' had begun to develop in their institutions a number of years ago. They saw it as a major factor behind their school's recent improvements in performance. Their dating of such developments was, however, rather imprecise because, as far as most of them were concerned, there had not really been a specific point at which what were now identified as the relevant initiatives could be said to have been launched. The nearest we have to such a key date is the arrival of Mrs Jameson at Park but, even in this case, quite a few staff clearly nursed aspirations for change in the months running up to her arrival at the school. At both schools the 'focus on achievement' is best viewed as the culmination of a number of separate strands of development. Only rather late in the day had it become a unifying principle (a rallying cry) and a set of activities which staff could describe and articulate.

Reforming the mission and building an ethos

Four out of five staff at Park felt that the changes over the last five years in the 'ethos of the school' had been 'substantial'. Half the staff at Compton reported the same thing. Such a change was seen, at both schools, as an 'improvement' in its own right and also as a contributory factor to other developments.

Members of the SMTs in both schools saw themselves as being responsible for 'the ethos'. When they talked about it they tended to mention things like 'recognizing and celebrating achievement', 'a willingness to assume responsibility' and fostering 'co-operative and productive relationships'. They were aware, however, as they talked, of how their descriptions seemed rather vague; dates were more difficult to establish and effects more difficult to pin down.

Several strands come together regarding the ways in which the two schools attempted to develop the pupil ethos. Central to the process were the structures of rewards and sanctions and the allocation of pupil responsibilities.

The schools recognized the importance of rewarding good behaviour, not only through praise but also by awarding merit stamps which were affixed in the pupil planner. Merits were aggregated to give certificates of different value and eventually led to the award of small prizes (pens, key-rings, record vouchers). Such a reward system was, however, widely believed to diminish in its effectiveness as pupils got older. A Park pupil said:

> Merits are mainly for the younger pupils. Older pupils are not so worried about them. . . . Mrs Smith has realised we're not interested and is trying to think of something else.

Pupil achievements were celebrated publicly. For example, staff at Compton nominated pupils as 'achiever of the term' and (the ultimate accolade) 'achiever of the year'. Both schools also had formal presentation evenings at which GCSE certificates were awarded.

The schools' codes of classroom conduct, referred to in the previous section, with their various sanctions, were thought to have contributed to an improvement in discipline. One of Park's pupils told us:

> Pupils usually abide by the code of conduct. It's a good idea. If you don't keep to it, teachers stamp down on you very quickly.

Both schools had introduced a report card system for pupil misconduct. In Compton this took the form of a hierarchy of coloured cards success- ively issued if improvement failed to occur. Beyond the 'red' stage a pupil might be put on 'contract' and ultimately excluded. However, the system was not without problems. A Compton teacher remarked:

> Once a group of children have gone through the card system, they realize not a lot can happen. The system has to be seen to work quicker. . . . Some children flout the school rules consistently but the links with parents are good to let them know about the problem.

A pupil or school council existed in both institutions (and also year councils at Compton) as a means of involving pupils in the running of the school. The Compton school council was generally seen as effect- ive by most pupils 'because Bob Drake "actions" things – he goes to the headteacher and arranges action'. Other ways of involving pupils included 'hosts for the day' (a pair of pupils acting as first contact point for visitors to the school). A variant of this at Park had pupils working in the school office sorting mail and receiving telephone calls before the start of the school day. In addition, Park had introduced a prefect system and found it had had a beneficial effect on pupil behaviour.

The school assembly was seen, at least by the SMTs, as a means of reinforcing ethos. A head of department at Park commented on some of the changes which had occurred:

> The school assembly, which has a religious element, has an effect on how pupils regard the school. Mention is usually made of hard work, the achievements of sports teams. Awards are presented – the certificates given and the headteacher [affirms] that this is a good school.

Pupils, however, sometimes saw the purpose of assemblies in rather dif- ferent terms:

> Assembly is a waste of time. They stand up and tell a story with a moral in it. Boring. Waste of time.

All of the initiatives described above were brought together at Compton in a detailed staff compendium designated the code of practice. This presented a set of procedures which staff were expected to apply consist- ently. The code had emerged, in its most recent form, during the period under review. Its existence was quite frequently mentioned by those we interviewed. Its genesis, however, was to be found in a more limited code of conduct introduced in the late 1980s in response to growing concerns about pupil behaviour. It had been developed into its more comprehensive form in 1991 and further elaborated over the years. The development of the code had involved the participation of staff in various working parties, and Bob Drake was widely regarded as the force behind it. Indeed, several staff mentioned their involvement in working parties as one of the ways in which Compton had been run differently in recent years. It may be that in the formulation and reformulation of the code the staff had initially found some common ground. Whatever the reality, it is striking that at Compton it was frequently mentioned.

Changing management

Developing a 'new ethos' for staff was seen as important. How staff feel about their school will in part be influenced by how they are treated by their colleagues, particularly by those who form the SMT. Both management teams seemed increasingly aware of the messages sent out by their own styles and structures.

At Park the style of the SMT had been perceived, as Mrs Jameson put it, as 'paternalistic' and 'autocratic' by an 'unempowered' staff. Her intention was to change this perception. At her very first staff meeting she took the opportunity to demonstrate this by simply rearranging the chairs to form a circle. But she faced more serious problems. On taking up her post she had experienced some difficulty in working effectively with the existing deputies. One soon left, however, to take a post elsewhere and the other retired. This enabled two new appointments to be made. Within a fairly short time, then, of her arrival an entirely new SMT, committed to change, was in place.

At Compton the SMT had, in the past, been marked by personality clashes between the deputies. Many people in the school felt this had adversely affected the pace of development. During the last five years, however, two had retired in successive years and this had provided both the opportunity and the occasion for a restructuring of the SMT's responsibilities. Interestingly, it was only at this relatively late stage that Drake achieved formal status as an assistant head. In both schools staff pointed to the formation of a 'like-minded' SMT as an important development. Both SMTs were now regarded by staff as being 'more visible', 'open', 'consultative' and 'accessible'. A teacher reported:

> There is a willingness to improve how the school is perceived. It doesn't go on behind closed doors. Staff are involved through a series of working groups on codes of practice, etc.

The new SMT at Park was part of a larger reorganization of management structures and responsibilities. An important aspect of this was to bridge what was considered an unhelpful pastoral–academic divide. This resulted in three internal appointments of 'key stage managers'. The role of the Key Stage 3 and Key Stage 4 managers was to co-ordinate and support the work of the form tutors in their respective key stages. These arrangements were also reflected in the job descriptions of the new deputies, each of whom had overall responsibility for a key stage.

The second aspect of the reorganization reflected the fact that Mrs Jameson felt she had inherited a school characterized by an absence of staff meetings and a 'top-down approach to management with little involvement from teachers. A regular system of staff meetings, organized on a 'workshop basis', was introduced, along with a cycle of team meetings concerned with such things as: the key stages; pupil development; primary liaison; staff development; and subject departments. Greater emphasis was placed on conducting effective meetings. Staff we interviewed welcomed these changes and felt both that they were now more involved in running the school and that they had a greater sense of purpose and direction. A head of department told us:

> Five years ago it was quite oppressive; now more staff are involved through working groups and policy structures. There is a proper structure for ideas – it is not top-down. There are more meetings and these help to make the school run better. People know how things work and have more of a sense of direction.

Compton was not felt, at least as far as its SMT was concerned, to be in need of a major reorganization. The basic management structure had remained largely unchanged over the last five years. However, one change was noticeable – the SMT deliberately sought to involve more staff in decision-making, mainly through voluntary participation in working parties associated with particular policies and practices.

Changing departments

Much of the thinking in the two SMTs focused on what could be done to change particular departments. In both schools the subject departments were seen as relatively autonomous, with their own distinctive cultures. This meant that achieving a common mission across departments was a difficult task. The departments were seen, as one teacher commented, as 'the real engines of the school'. To pursue the analogy further, they were engines which could often run at different speeds – some at full throttle and some barely ticking over at all.

An explicit strategy for departmental improvement seems necessary if a school is to improve across the board. Thinking in the two schools appears to have proceeded along the following lines:

• Appoint a new head of department when the occasion arises.
• Assume that school-wide initiatives will bring about departmental improvement.

- Disseminate the practice of 'well-running' departments to others.
- Develop the 'ticking over' departments with the help of external support.

In practice, the two schools mainly concentrated on the first and second of these two strategies. Their thinking and practice in relation to the third and fourth were still developing.

In both schools the planning process had become more systematic and formalized. This was particularly apparent at Park, where the brevity and imprecision of the 1990 'management plan' was in marked contrast to the latest detailed and comprehensive version, with its clear link to the school's aims and further analyses of targets, tasks and responsibilities. A head of department at Park told us that the new school plan was now seen as the practical embodiment of the school's vision:

> There is a clear vision, repeated often. Staff meetings are an open forum at which there is always reference to the school plan. She [Mrs Jameson] has a grip on where things fit into the plan – the plan is realistic and achievable.

It is worth noting that when some of our interviewees tried to summarize what had occurred in their institutions it was rather easier to say what had changed for staff than for pupils. Staff *had* noticed, for example, that the chairs had been rearranged at staff meetings; more staff were aware that they were being involved in working parties to formulate school policies; management structures had been revamped to make responsibilities more explicit; and so on. Corresponding accounts of what had changed for pupils were rather vaguer. What seemed to matter was the broader picture to which the 'fine details' pointed. Underlying the changes in both schools was the feeling that something more wide-ranging and important was afoot. Such sentiments were evident in both schools, but perceptions were stronger at Park than at Compton.

Working on the image

Government policy has put schools directly into competition with one another. Aspects of image management had consequently become a key concern for both headteachers. The support of the parent body (and the potential parent body) needed to be secured to ensure the continued financial viability and future of their schools. Both had, as a result, started a number of initiatives.

Developing good relationships with parents had become a commitment for the SMTs. In both schools parental views had been sought by questionnaire surveys and the findings had been influential – as evidenced, for example, in the development of Compton's code of practice.

The importance of not merely courting but engaging with parents was underlined by the schools' commitment to home–school partnerships. The obligations of each of the three partners – teachers, parents and pupils – in meeting the aims of the school were set out. In both schools a significant improvement in recent years in the frequency and quality of the communication between teachers and parents was perceived to have taken place. This change was perhaps most marked at Park, where previously no individual teacher had been allowed to phone out and everything had gone through the deputy head.

Presenting the school in the 'right light' to parents and the public generally had clearly become an increasing preoccupation. Many of the initiatives already described helped to foster a positive image. Others given particular attention included: a renewed commitment to school uniform (after consultation with pupils and parents); development of the parent–teacher association and further links with local businesses, colleges and other organizations; courting the local press (the 'anti-Compton' bias of a local newspaper had been successfully overcome); and more frequent school 'open days'.

More effort had also been put into primary school liaison. The Key Stage 2/3 manager at Park school had been influential in fostering links with feeder primary schools. It was recognized that it was not enough to focus on the final year (Year 6) of the primary schools and liaison was therefore extended to include Year 5. Meanwhile, the loss of some able primary pupils to a neighbouring secondary school had prompted the organization of extension classes for a small number of high-flyers who came to Park for an hour a week over 18 months. Other activities had also been encouraged: a roadshow, taster days, and staff two-way visits. These efforts had resulted in increasing pupil numbers in Year 7: the intake had risen from around 70 to over 100, the largest intake to the school for ten years.

Finally, both had given some attention to the appearance of the school. They had been able to carry out major programmes of improvement to their accommodation, facilities and resources. These were invariably cited with approval when we asked Year 11 pupils how the schools had changed in the previous five years. Keeping the schools attractive and tidy had undoubtedly been a major concern, and both claimed success in reducing the amount of litter and graffiti. A considerable amount of energy had gone into building up both schools' images. One Park pupil said:

Before we came the school didn't have a very good reputation. But my parents say it has got much better and is now one of the best schools round here.

Sustaining the pace

It is difficult to judge just how fast staff in the two schools were running. What is clear is that most staff *felt* they were running faster than a few years previously. When we talked to them they mentioned the kinds of stresses and strains that anyone who has been a teacher during the 1990s is likely to recognize. We had expected the pace of change to cause additional problems. Interestingly, we did not find much evidence that this was the case in these two schools – teachers in other schools were more stressed, in our view.

None the less, questions about whether staff could keep up their present efforts loomed large in both schools. A good part of what they were doing (probably the larger part) depended on teachers' being willing to work beyond the contractual requirements of their jobs. Could this extra commitment be sustained over further long periods of time? And should it be expected without financial or other recognition following in its wake?

Concluding comments

The improvement efforts at Park and Compton emerged from very different starting-points and backgrounds. Each had built up its own 'natural history' of change. Despite these differences, both schools finished up with a set of initiatives which were strikingly similar. Joyce (1991) refers to the process of improvement as one of 'opening doors'. Quite a number, it would seem from these two cases, have to be opened before evidence of improvement starts to emerge.

The door of 'teaching and learning' is arguably one of the most important. It appears that these two schools were seeking to open this door mainly by reinforcing and extending traditional supports for teaching and learning (Wilcox 1997). More recently, professional development had begun to focus on 'effective learning' (at Compton) and teaching and learning styles (at Park). Again, history and context are important here. Even the (re)discovery of the value of pupils having their own copies of textbooks may seem novel to a generation of teachers brought up on the ubiquitous worksheet.

Going through the doors successfully does not guarantee that the process of improvement necessarily continues on course. Slavin (1995) argues that schools have to make a number of choices about how they will proceed. The notion of schools making active choices about their change strategies does not quite fit the positions at Compton and Park. What both schools do seem to have done is find ways of working with which they were comfortable. To date these have served them reasonably well. Many of the challenges they faced have proved surmountable and there has been enough 'success' in the early stages to sustain the action. They both felt they had largely 'done it by themselves'.[1] However, both saw potential difficulties lying ahead. These included: the loss of key staff; external threats of increased competition; budgetary cuts and even possible closure. In neither case was the inheritance felt to be entirely secure.

Note

1 Interestingly, both these schools were in LEAs whose advisory/inspection teams placed considerable importance on 'helping schools to help themselves'.

 **7**

A SIMPLE CASE OF
LEADERSHIP

Blackstone School is located in a town which has been economically depressed for a long time. The closure of the town's coalmines some years ago was the latest blow in a long-term pattern of economic decline. The school had turned comprehensive in the 1970s but had had difficulty shaking off its 'secondary modern' past. It did not attract the most able pupils in its catchment area and was associated by many in its community with a lack of opportunities – other comprehensives in the locality were more popular and more successful.

When Mark Barney took over as headteacher, the school's exam results (like the community in which it was located) were languishing. He launched himself into the task of turning the school around, making it clear to all who would listen that the school needed to be improved. In the process he initiated a number of simple reforms.

The recognition that there was under-performance had been masked to some extent by low expectations, both among the community and among some of the school's staff. In the terms of this study Blackstone was initially of 'less than average effectiveness'. Over the period we covered, however, it began to 'improve rapidly'. Indeed, by the time of our fieldwork it was beginning to nudge ahead of the pack.[1]

New leadership, new attitudes

Everyone we spoke to agreed that the key change at Blackstone was the appointment of its new head. Indeed, even Barney himself, in answer to a question on the importance of his role, observed that he was 'pivotal'. He said:

I see myself as being the inspiration of the school to have moved forward and to continue to move forward. I see myself as a facilitator in enabling my colleagues to move themselves, the school and the pupils in a direction which I have dictated.

The head of lower school echoed Barney's description of his contribution:

most people know that Mark Barney has clear views on what he wants and that if he says that's what going to happen, then clearly they know that that is going to be the case.

Summarizing what he had done at the school, Barney elaborated:

I would love to say that it came from the parents, I would love to say it came from the kids, I'd love to say it came from the governors, I'd love to say it came from the staff, but, at the end of the day, it came from me. I've driven it, taken people with me, got them on board, but there's no question about where it came from. . . . I've had support, please don't think I haven't had support. My senior staff – met all of them. You can see how they have helped enorm-ously but . . . with somebody else at the figurehead they would have done the same, provided they had similar views. It's not me that's done it – but there's no question, the push, the drive, has come from me. I stood up on the soap box and I have said we're going to do it, that's it.

Barney's directness was in marked contrast to that of the previous head, a man who had been appointed in the mid-1970s to merge the three local secondary modern schools. A 'liberal educator' by disposition, this head had dismantled some of the earlier hallmarks of the grammar school tradition (including such things as school uniform). In the context of what now needed to be done, Barney's strength was that he was not at all like his predecessor. He gained from the comparisons.

The school was seen by some of the older staff to have developed an innovation-oriented ethos but also to have lacked the management drive to implement changes. As one teacher put it:

There was an air of frustration, there was an air of acceptance. There were innovations that were brought on board and dropped without seeing them through, things happening that they weren't happy with. They [the staff] were desperate, I think, for somebody to say, here's a direction – let's all move in it. And here's some rope – let's go and see if we can hang ourselves with it.

The head of English gave a similar diagnosis, pointing out that the new head had released the staff from some of their frustrations under the old regime:

People had responsibilities and that before. You see we had a staff – when the change of head came about – we had a staff who'd been getting disgruntled and frustrated for a couple of years before because they felt, they were concerned about things like discipline and appearance, they were concerned about things and they wanted things to happen and they quite often felt that any tightening up that they wanted to do wasn't necessarily supported. They needed support, they needed to know that somebody else was behind them, prepared to actually back them in what they were doing. Of course when Mark came and had a different attitude, such a different person from the previous head, they felt then that because he had this streak of hardness as well as his understanding side, they felt that they could do things and they would be backed. I think that's the thing. I think particularly [in dealing] with parents, they felt they would get the backing that they needed.

Challenging pupil behaviour patterns

Under Barney staff were encouraged to 'take a stand' and deal with pupils' misbehaviour and misdemeanours. This was in marked contrast to the attitude of 'turning a blind eye' which had previously prevailed. One of the 'line teachers' described how matters had been dealt with in the past:

Nobody ever went out on a limb because they knew they wouldn't get any support. Nobody actually felt secure to handle situations. They had no confidence, either to handle the situation and to pass it on or to pass it on without handling it. There was no real strong bond between senior management and the rest of the teaching staff so things started to . . . come out of the hedges, you know. Kids would be walking round and nobody would ever challenge them and say why not, in an accusatory way, but just enquire as to why five lads were all horsing around and nobody was bothering about it. You know when I first came here people would sort of . . . disappear, they'd think, well I'll pretend I don't see that, and it's not a problem. And what they did was they . . . retrenched into their classroom. They thought this is my domain, I'll look after it, I'm not going outside but I know I'm safe in here. So some of the older staff, I felt when I first arrived, were quite dismissive of senior management, quite cynical.

The staff felt discipline had improved as a result of the adoption of clear guidelines about appropriate sanctions and the ways in which punishments would be enforced. As the head explained:

There's a very firm discipline within the school, very firm, the children know exactly where they are. Typical things are, if a child swears in school they go home. If a child thumps another child in school they go home. If a child is caught smoking in school they will have five minutes with teachers and on the second occasion they will go home and every child in school knows those things.

This no-nonsense approach to discipline was the platform from which other strategies were launched.

Tackling achievement

Barney's 'new regime' concentrated on attempting to improve academic achievement. As he put it:

I'm sure that they're nice kids. I'm not a parent of my own, I don't have children of my own, I have over 700 here and I'm told, and I'm sure it's true and I do believe this, the children are not nice through accident. They may well be basically nice, [but] factors in life tend to make them not on the whole. Our kids are nice kids. That is what is so important for Blackstone School, we have nice kids who behave, who work hard and are proud to be associated with all of those things and particularly proud of their own achievements. They do well, they're praised for it, they like the praise, they feed on it, it does them good.

The importance of upping levels of academic achievement had been a constant refrain from the time of Barney's appointment. In addition to the benefits for pupils, his reasoning was twofold – improved results would give the school a better image in the eyes of parents and help to 'claw back' some of the children from the school's historic catchment areas who were 'leaking' into rival schools.

There was a realization among the SMT that the school had hitherto been concentrating unduly on 'non-academic' matters. By way of example, the deputy head told us they had counted the number of rewards at morning assembly for different types of activity and had been appalled to discover that over 75 per cent of them were for sporting achievements. An attempt to improve the balance between academic and other areas followed, with additional attention being given to getting homework in on time. At the same time, as with other schools in this study, Blackstone embarked on the 'usual' initiatives (entering pupils for more exams, reviewing the choice of exam boards and so on).

In addition, the school focused upon its merit system. A mixture of intrinsic and extrinsic rewards was used to bring about improvements in achievement in both academic and non-academic spheres. As one of the teachers of French outlined:

> We have a merit system in Years 7 and 8 where any good piece of work, whether it's homework, classwork or whatever, the child picks up a commendation. So many commendations make a merit, so many merits you get a book token. In the upper school in Years 9, 10 and 11 we have termly awards where all staff are invited to nominate pupils from their teaching groups who have either improved or have been the highest achievers. And what we do then is anybody who gets more than two nominations in various subjects gets a letter of commendation sent home to parents. Those who actually get the greatest number of commendations, in Year 9 they receive a £5 gift token, in Year 10 a £10 gift token and in Year 11 a £15 gift token, and this is per term. So there's three sets of awards per year. In addition to that, a lot of the individual subjects have awards and certificates. Science operates an award scheme. Humanities operates an award scheme as well.

Changing attitudes among middle management

At Barney's insistence, the academic organization of the school was over-hauled. An enhanced role was given to the heads of faculties, who had previously been a part of the general system of drift and demoralization that had beset the school. As the deputy head explained:

> So step one was just . . . was dead easy, which is basically, we've got the heads of faculty to run their faculties the way we wanted. And what we tried to do basically is to give as much responsibility to them as we possibly can and then to meet them regularly to discuss it and in return for the freedom to make them accountable. So we have regular meetings with these managers who are regarded as being responsible for both the day-to-day and for the long-term strategic planning of their area. We've given them freedom to decide who, when, where, what, with what, and said to them go away with our support and deliver it. But they're left in no doubt that the primary function of them being here is to deliver a quality curric-ulum in the areas that they have responsibility for and that that is demonstrated in a number of different ways. It's demonstrated not just in GCSE results – which clearly needed to be improved – but it's also demonstrated in how many students are entered for GCSE.

In addition to both decentralizing power and holding middle manage-ment accountable for the use of that power, the school joined one of the national value-added systems designed to show whether departments were performing above or below the expectations for them. The introduction of this sort of information into the school was initially explosive. The deputy head recounted what happened when the data on their 'effectiveness' was handed out to staff:

I'll never forget, the day before the last day of term. The shit hit the fan. There were people running round slamming these things on desks saying 'And what's this? I know nothing about it!' It was simply – this is a system that we'd like to introduce, we think it's a very important management tool. It's a management tool not designed to nail your arse to the mast but to be used as a productive and constructive way of analysing examination results. We have done it for last year just so that you can flick and peruse and stick it on your desk for you to have a look at but we will be using this next year.... We had a very interesting 48 hours, and at one point there was a very heavy push by heads of faculty to stick it where the sun don't shine and not to use it. But then we had Easter and everybody sort of chilled out and went to Tenerife for their holidays and came back and they were at the next meeting and it was, 'Are we going to use that?'. Yes. That was it. And it ... signalled to people that there was a change of ethos, that in return they were going to have to be more accountable, they were going to have to be more directly responsible. The other thing that it signalled more than anything else is that, really for the first time, the senior management team actually had the information that they needed to make the school better.

Changes in management arrangements were paralleled by an attempt to develop a more 'inclusive' climate of relations between the head and the staff. Barney both increased the number of meetings of sub-units within the school (faculty, year, department) and attempted to operate an 'open door' policy for staff with a view to showing his willingness to listen to staff opinions.

Building the image

Blackstone's image in its local community had been poor for some while. As part of a process of 'image management' the school introduced a policy whereby children were stopped from going into the local town at lunch-times. As a member of the English Department told us:

We've done a very positive [public relations] job. One of the first things we did, for instance, is that in lunch hours all kids were allowed out of school and what used to happen then, you'd have big gangs of kids ... going down to town and if you actually drive down [there] you can see that the pavements are narrow and so forth. You'd have . . . twenty or thirty kids in waves going down . . . milling around town and then coming back, so you used to get all these . . . comments. Oh no, the kids are allowed out, they're not supervised. So one of the first things we did was that we banned everybody from going out unless they actually lived in [the town] and had gone home for dinner.

The school's campaign to improve its image in the local community was extended in other ways as well. A school uniform was introduced, along with a new emphasis on 'pride in the school'. A focused public relations campaign, led by the appointment of a member of staff as the school 'press/public relations person', was also instituted.

There was one other change which a knowledgeable visitor to the school might have noticed. Barney abolished the bells that used to sound at the end of each lesson. A senior teacher told us about the change:

I mean, one of the most tangible things that makes Blackstone different to them [the pupils] is the fact that we have no bells and therefore there isn't this cacophony of noise and movement which in many ways aggravates and irritates the kids because they're having to push and shove and jostle. There are no bells so in fact the movement around the school is much easier because it's slightly staggered – the advantage is that it's quieter. We are now going through a period change. It's not noisy, it's not loud, it's not a cacophony. You put a bell in and everybody has to talk over the bell and it stirs everybody up.

Getting round to learning?

All the changes Barney introduced were pragmatic ones; they were not informed by 'educational commitments' of any kind. How far changes to the organizational arrangements at Blackstone impacted on activities at the classroom level is a moot point. As the head noted, in explaining the consequences of some of his reforms:

I thought there would be quite substantial improvements in the quality of teaching and learning in school. I thought it would be because our children achieved more in more areas. They are happier in what they're doing in many areas of their work, therefore it follows (I thought) that the quality of teaching them had improved. It must have because the examination results . . . have improved out of all proportion, [while] the ability of the children at intake hasn't. But I'm not convinced that's the case. I think what's happened is that people are being more focused in what they're teaching and therefore in the learning of the children. Nobody's improving quality. In fact it might have dropped . . . in some areas.

Many of the teachers we spoke to were also uncertain how far the changes had penetrated classrooms. One teacher told us:

Certainly quality of teaching and learning has improved, but I wouldn't say that it was a substantial change, [but] between moderate and substantial.

Another added:

I wouldn't say that we've really yet got to a learning culture and I would say to a certain extent that hasn't changed a great deal at all. The climate of the school has certainly changed. I mean that goes along with the pupils' behaviour and I think the fact that staff accept, realize that they're going to be supported in terms of discipline and so on. A lot of it I think is almost on the face of it. It's changed, and certainly the kids look better. Discipline is better.

While Barney himself was sceptical about the extent of changes in classroom practices he felt that he had facilitated a greater consistency of approach across the school. It was this, rather than a change of methods, which had contributed to the improvement. When asked what, in his view, was the key thing, he referred to the 'stick of rock' factor:

you probably know the stick of rock syndrome where you break the stick of rock and wherever you break it, it always says the same. . . . That's what I tried to do, consistency right the way through from the humblest headteacher to the most important class teacher in the school, from the lunch-time supervisor to the school secretary, the caretaker, the governors, visitors to the school. This is what I call ethos. It's about setting out what you want and then developing it. We have got nice kids; nice kids are not nice kids by nature.

Concluding thoughts

In many ways Blackstone had pursued, under Barney's leadership, a quite unsophisticated model of improvement, especially in comparison with some of the more wide-ranging efforts that had been made elsewhere. One obvious difference was that it had concentrated mainly on school-level changes – intervention at the 'learning level' had been minimal. But even at the school-wide level there were differences – what Barney had orchestrated was the pulling of *simple* levers for change. They covered pupil behaviour, attitudes towards academic achievement and patterns of middle management. By focusing the agenda in this way, Barney had also succeeded in reducing considerably the range of responses among a staff group which had previously exhibited (and been allowed to exhibit) wide variations in values, behaviours and strategies.

Blackstone serves an essentially working-class area with historically low educational expectations. Barney seized the moment, offered a much clearer sense of direction to the staff and concentrated on implementing a small number of changes. Given the school's context and recent history, this 'simple approach' seems to have worked. The deputy head offered support for this view:

> I think the greatest advantage – to be honest – in the turnaround, it was very easy because there were a group of people here who were virtually stable staff who wanted the senior management team to do something, to get off their arses, to get out of their offices and to help them. The staff knew what was wrong, the staff knew how to fix it, they just wanted somebody who took an assembly and had responsibility for it to just help them. You know in many ways this school was ripe to be turned round because everybody wanted it. The vast proportion of kids knew that it was falling out at the edges, the majority of staff knew that it was just a crock and that nobody was getting anything out of it . . . and the parents were in support.

Barney's direct and straightforward approach to leadership fitted the problems which had emerged at Blackstone. He offered the energy and commitment the school needed to get out of its rut. The school and its immediate community could, as a result, face the future with greater confidence.

Note

1 In the year after our fieldwork finished, however, this 'rapid improvement' tailed off.

8

MOVING (AND STAYING) AHEAD

Highdale and Rowland were both schools which had improved rapidly over the last five years. Highdale's improvement had been from a base of 'average effectiveness', while Rowland had continued to improve from a position of 'above average effectiveness'. Both schools stood out, however, in our study for another equally important reason – namely, the extent to which teachers reported changes in the 'quality of teaching and learning'.

Well over half the staff at Rowland told us there had been 'substantial' changes in the quality of teaching and learning over the last five years. While this figure may seem low in comparison with some of the other changes which teachers reported had taken place, it was a good deal higher than in any other school. At Highdale the comparable figure was considerably under half. Again, however, this was a relatively high proportion in comparison with other schools.

Highdale is an 11–16 school serving a large market town. Having initially opened as a secondary modern school, it turned comprehensive in the late 1970s and takes most of the children in its area. In addition, and largely as a result of its good reputation, it draws pupils from outside its official catchment. Its pupils are drawn from varied social and economic backgrounds; the proportion on free school meals (which was less than one-in-five) is around the national average, while over 5 per cent are 'statemented'.

Rowland is also an 11–16 school, but this status is more recent and results from the LEA's decision to set up a post-16 institution in the area in the early 1990s. It, too, is situated in a market town but its intake is relatively advantaged in terms of social background, with only around 10 per cent on free school meals.

Talking about teaching

The message at both schools was basically similar. As one deputy head put it, 'It's OK to talk about teaching'. An English teacher at Highdale, for example, recounted 'an interesting experiment':

> I have a class which is mixed ability but with the top set removed. Normally I would have had lower expectations of this class than of a top set. This year I decided to expect the same of them as of the top set – and they have risen to the occasion! They are achieving at a much higher level than I would have thought possible. . . . Recently, when we were doing a Shakespeare play, I gave them a choice of five pieces of writing to do. The first was an essay (compare/contrast) on which they could get an A and I would not normally expect this class to tackle it. On the other titles they could get perhaps a C. I explained all this – what was involved – and allowed them to choose what one to do. An amazing number chose the essay and are tackling it very well and some will get an A. Before they would not have had the opportunity in this group to achieve this grade and I felt very guilty about that.

Teachers at Rowland spoke of curricular changes with equal enthusiasm. A member of the information technology (IT) department at Rowland described how a major innovation had developed at the school:

> We call it all 'Curriculum Plus'.[1] I suppose it really started off as an IT course in Year 7. I've always thought ever since I've been here that the sort of IT kit that we've got is very good and that the youngsters were amazing in terms of their skills. . . . the time to do it is in Year 7, to get them all to the same level was my initial philosophy. So I created space in Year 7 to put in an IT course to guarantee certain skills. It was done partly in the timetable and then audited as cross-curricular in certain areas of design – science did it as well, maths did. We knew elsewhere that those were the three that were particularly monitored to enjoy a certain level of IT competence . . . The conversation really went from there: 'Hang on, what about IT, what about numeracy and literacy?' That then blossomed into Curriculum Plus which then was enhanced through the use of things like Successmaker.[2] . . . And then we went from Year 7 to Year 8.

The role that technology had played at Rowland in encouraging change was also picked up by the head of music:

> I would say there's a much greater emphasis on the use of techno-logy, a much greater emphasis. That applies pretty much to every subject, I would imagine, and the use of computers to actually help

differentiation, instead of a teacher who might try to differentiate
. . . obviously the computer can actually target the exact level that is
necessary.

Given that the school had recently received funds to support technology-
related developments, this interest is not surprising. But there were also
many other indications that teaching was a frequent topic for discussion
among the staff at Rowland. One told us about a recent conversation:

> I spoke to another member of staff recently who told me about
> an English lesson he'd done and he was telling me . . . it was a Year
> 8 group and they'd actually been studying a Shakespeare play and
> they wanted to recreate a storm with the Shakespeare text spoken
> above the storm, so he actually used the pupils as resources them-
> selves to create the sound of the wind and rain and all this business,
> while the others had to read out the script on top of that. So obvi-
> ously they started getting a bit timid and a bit shy, then he built up
> the wind and the rain, got them going, so they had to actually shout
> it so they got the passion of what was required. All of that before
> they really understood. The actual learning hadn't quite taken place
> at that point.

Describing the swings over the years in the maths department, a teacher
at Highdale commented:

> in the last five years there has been a concerted attempt to get
> new approaches accepted by the department such as more talking
> in maths, more emphasis on discussion and proof and a move back
> towards structuring open tests.

He then went on to explain:

> Around 1980 pupils worked exclusively from textbooks; progress was
> measured by the number of pages a child covered. The class moved
> at a standard pace. 1984 to 1989 saw a move away from textbooks
> to teacher-generated work. This was perhaps too open-ended and
> became almost a free-for-all. From 1990 onwards we have concen-
> trated on making sure 'open-ended' doesn't mean 'total freedom' –
> so we have swung back to look at how open-ended approaches can
> be more structured. There is now more emphasis on core mathemat-
> ical processes for doing things and activities rather than doing them
> for fun.

There had been similar trends in other departments such as geography
and science. A science teacher said:

> Our way of tackling investigations has changed for the better. We
> now think more about findings and there is less chalk and talk. We
> get the children to think more.

The head of geography was also concerned to make stronger connections between elements of pupils' learning:

> Because of better planning the delivery in the classroom is of a higher quality – ideas and resources are shared more and there is more evaluation. There is a more reflective approach – looking at what happens in other departments, learning from our mistakes. This is true of departments generally. Sometimes we plan with other departments. For example, in a topic on 'birds of prey' we were interested in why they were becoming extinct and the technology department [was interested] in the construction of owl boxes.

Discussions about teaching were not, however, simply confined to the formal curriculum. The head of physical education at Rowland told us that a deliberate attempt had been made to involve a higher proportion of pupils in extra-curricular activities, even though the school had made considerable efforts in this area already. Citing the changes in the PE department, he explained:

> We found a number of ways of targeting a larger number of kids. . . . We've looked broader across the school. A lot of the events we run we would now consider as whole-school events. For example, we run a sports day and basically every kid competes in that, it's an eight-hour business, whereas the old thing was of two people from each group competing on behalf of their group. . . . and we've tried to accommodate areas which are broadly physical education (like outdoor pursuits) into broader school events. The PE department would now be considered as more of an integral part of the whole school.

Staff in both schools were aware that they had been encouraged to engage in professional dialogues about teaching and learning. However, while such perceptions were widely shared, teachers differed about how well established they were. Pondering on the changes which had occurred at Rowland, the head of English said:

> I don't know whether it's been motivated by Ofsted or not, but I feel that the head's priorities have increasingly become what actually happens in the classroom and that focuses on teaching and learning.

Another teacher in the same school said:

> I would say the increased focus in lessons and on the quality of teaching and learning and on the consistency of pupils' experiences probably occurred within the last 18 months.

This realization that 'something' was happening turned out to be relatively recent among other staff as well. The practice of 'talking about teaching' had preceded their awareness of its importance.

The management of learning

By 1995 the notion of the 'management of learning' had become sufficiently central at Highdale to be made one of the corner-stones of the
school's development plan. The main elements of this plan involved:
extending the role of middle managers within the school; the continu-
ing promotion of professional dialogues about learning; further clarifica-
tion of the role of the SMT as managers of learning; and a renewed focus
on the tutorial system.

While the incorporation of such concerns into the plan was relatively
new, the thinking behind them stretched back to the end of the 1980s.
Very deliberate efforts had, in fact, been made to get the various departments talking more about teaching and learning. Describing some of the
changes which had kicked the school into action, the head of science
said:

> There was a strong lead from Sam Purchiss [one of the assistant
> heads] to look at the quality of teaching through meetings and the
> use of speakers for INSET – this opened minds.

Purchiss confirmed this account. Departments had been encouraged to
identify people outside the school they thought might be important
to their development, as well as the issues they wanted to discuss, and
got 'people of national stature to talk about these things'. More recently
a small, invited group of staff had worked through materials from the
Open University about attitudes and beliefs towards children as learners.

At the same time the school had sought out additional help with some
of its developments. It had, for example, been a very active participant
in the LEA's value-added project. Maths INSET in the LEA was also popular and felt to be of high quality. The advisory service had worked alongside teachers and created materials to respond to schools' needs which
Highdale had subsequently taken up. In addition, a former LEA maths
adviser had now gone freelance and the school had employed him to
teach two days a week as well as getting further INSET from him.

The school had also made a special effort to think through how new
appointees were inducted. New staff had not always understood what
the practical activities prescribed by the schemes of work, for example,
were intended for. As one head of department told us:

> We didn't appreciate or anticipate how difficult this would be for
> new staff. We hoped that it would all be transmitted by word of
> mouth. It obviously wasn't.

Two or three other changes were also identified as key reforms. One of
these had been the attempt to 'open up classroom doors'. As the head
put it:

Staff now teach with doors open and the head can enter classrooms and be welcomed. The aim is to support people professionally so we have department suites with lots of places to meet and develop healthy dialogues.

To reinforce this process of connecting with classroom practice, the SMT had tried to look at pupils' work each week as a team and then see those concerned to give comments and commendations. This approach had, in turn, involved individual departments in having regular meetings to identify the 'best work of the week'. At the same time a concerted effort had been made to get more discussion going about what was actually happening in classrooms. A teacher told us:

A major change was the introduction of the monitoring of pupils' learning through classroom visits.

Allied to this had been a major rethinking of the role of the special educational needs support staff. A learning support teacher explained:

In learning support we have gone back to what we always believed was right, that is to have a support centre in which small groups of very weak children spend short periods. They have classroom support as well. . . . We go into classrooms and plan support for some children within classrooms.

Finding the right balance between in-class support and separate provision had not, however, been easy. This teacher was not convinced that the system that had emerged was 'completely effective'. The head, however, reported that the special educational needs staff had been an important component of the 'opening doors' policy (the only departments which were not involved in this way were PE, art and technology) and that it was now 'common to have two teachers in a classroom'.

Learning at the centre

Developments at Rowland had followed a somewhat different course over the last five years, although there were clearly parallels. Its head was committed to creating a school which was 'a liberal institution with rigorous academic standards' and which 'assumes that most kids will behave perfectly reasonably most of the time and therefore treats them as if they will rather than as if they won't'. A strategy of devolving power to staff had been combined with attempts to redefine the role of the pupils. A deputy head expressed it in the following terms:

I think the school's ethos is one of its main distinctive features and something that's been arrived at through a process of consultation with staff and pupils. I think it's a strong ethos to have. In many

schools, where there's a 'them and us' situation, the teachers sometimes feel that break- and lunch-times are under siege, but there's
not that feeling here. It's very much an open school and it's the
pupils' school as much as it's the staff's school. It is a happy working
environment.

This theme was continued by the other deputy:

it's an enjoyable place to work in and it's a challenging place to
work in. Pupils and staff have high expectations of each other.

Pupils, in short, were expected to be 'powerful' – to be active, involved
and possibly critical of what the school was providing.

Developing this theme, a class teacher told us in another interview
about how some of these expectations got translated into colleagues'
thinking:

as a school we like to think of ourselves as being very forward thinking, so rather than delivering the National Curriculum in a rather
dry way, I think we try to find ways to really enthuse the pupils,
excite the pupils while obviously adhering to what the National
Curriculum requirements are. So we're actually bringing it to life as
much as possible.

The school's commitment to the 'learning level' had recently become
symbolized by the opening of a Learning Centre. For the SMT this was
seen as a way of ensuring the continuation of the improvement in the
quality of learning that had already been initiated by more conventional
mechanisms. Supported by a tranche of technology-related funds, the
Centre was situated at the physical heart of the school and incorporated
all the existing library provision, the integrated learning systems and
information and communication technology provision. While it was
acknowledged that the potential of these developments was still being
explored, enthusiasm about them ran high. Indeed, one teacher even told
us that their use was 'like having a one-to-one teacher–pupil relation'.

Changes in the learning environment at Highdale had been less obvious but were also in evidence. A Year 11 pupil told us, for example, that:

the library has got its act together. In our first year the books were
not good, the library was boring. Now there are good books for
lessons and you can watch videos there. It's now a relaxing place
to go.

However, while the school had undoubtedly secured general improvements, pupils still pointed to certain departments where equipment was
poor, textbooks were in short supply and basic materials were not always
available.

Restructuring middle management

The ways in which both schools were now tackling issues of teaching and learning give little hint of the turmoil which had preceded them. At Highdale almost all the staff said that there had been 'substantial' changes in the 'ways the school was run and organized', while at Rowland around four out of five reported in similar terms.

Headteacher Peter South's predecessor at Rowland felt he had taken the school as far as he could before taking early retirement. When South, a recently arrived deputy at the school, was appointed to the headship he was already very familiar with the pace of change which had been initiated and was keen to see it continued. However, while acknowledging the school's traditional strengths, he felt that several fundamental changes were required if the school was to continue to progress.

The previous head's management style had combined a degree of 'openness' and staff involvement with some 'push' from the centre, and this had changed little over the years. During his relatively short time at the school South had come to believe that important changes were being blocked. In the process he identified two main problems. First, the school was, in his view, too pastorally focused. And second, the collegiality of the staffroom had resulted in the formation of cliques. More energy for change was needed, but a means of circumventing 'blockages' in some departments was also required.

Inheriting a system of heads of year, subject and house, he had, within two years of taking over, embarked on an ambitious restructuring of middle management. In pursuit of a 'new' culture, he had taken a number of seemingly dramatic steps. These had included: closing the staffroom and stopping the year heads' and house heads' meetings as well as terminating the existing house system. In its place a new faculty structure had been created, with each of the faculties having devolved responsibility for the school's non-capita funding. At the same time a new pastoral/academic organization had been set up consisting of a head plus assistant at Key Stage 3 and a similar structure at Key Stage 4, with a separate Year 7 head.

The new faculty structure was staffed partly by internal promotions but was augmented with some 'new blood' from outside. The removal of the school's sixth form provided some unexpected room for manoeuvre here, as several older staff moved into the new tertiary college. In the process a new staff development policy also began to emerge. The faculty structure had opened up some opportunities and several ambitious young staff were attracted to the school with the promise that, if they stayed for four or five years, they would be helped to move on to promotions elsewhere.

During this period the school also changed its timetable, introducing a 'continuous day' system. Still further changes were envisaged, with moves towards a closer integration of the pastoral and academic systems in the pipeline.

Staff resistance to these changes seemed modest – they took most of them in their stride. What was interesting about the school was that there was a fairly widespread feeling that the new structures had encouraged a degree of innovation in curriculum provision, along with a degree of ownership. The previous head had undoubtedly encouraged some 'risk-taking' without making it central. In combination with the staff changes which he had been able to effect, it was a legacy South was to build upon.

Restructuring senior management

The changes at Highdale had been equally fundamental but had taken longer to emerge. When he took over as Highdale's head in the mid-1980s, John North had inherited an 'old guard' of three deputy heads and two senior teachers. They were 'delightful people', as he put it, but out of touch and sympathy with the wider changes which were increasingly affecting schools. Crucially, they continued to reflect the previous head's view that 'teachers should not talk about teaching'.

As we reconstructed what had happened at Highdale, it became clear that the foundations for the school's improvement had been laid in the period 1988–90 when North had already been in post for some two to three years. In the early years he had made few changes – 'just tinkering efforts', as he put it. He had encouraged some work on self-review, introduced a staff bulletin and organized a series of weekend conferences for teachers to get to know each other and establish some collective vision.

Meanwhile, some of the heads of department (and notably Purchiss and Johnson) were 'chafing at the bit' because of the apparent lack of direction in relation to teaching and learning. The frustration at head of department level led eventually to what Purchiss (now an assistant head) refers to as 'almost a coup'. Meeting at a residential conference, departmental heads produced a document which was not merely critical of the deputy head structure but emphasized their belief that the curriculum (and hence teaching and learning) should be at the centre of policy-making.

North was generally sympathetic to the views of the 'young Turks' and provided subtle support for their aspirations, but did not feel in a position to move immediately. As the implications of the 1988 Education Reform Act came to be played out, heads of department increasingly became the focus for innovative reform in the school. There was an uneasy period during which tensions between them and the deputies became more manifest. Over the next few years, however, opportunities arose, as a result of retirements among the SMT, for some radical restructuring.

A new SMT structure emerged consisting of the head and four assistant heads (all of whom were promoted internally from head of department roles). All four assistant heads have a 50 per cent teaching time-table alongside their other duties and three continue to act as heads of department.

The adoption of the dual assistant head/head of department role is a visible expression of the SMT's belief that the core task of a school is the management of teaching and learning and that heads of department should be at the centre of school management and policy functions. The previous system was felt to give primacy to pastoral matters, with heads of year prevailing. The Highdale structure is a distinct move away from the more common arrangement in which heads of department are account-able to a curriculum deputy. The substantial teaching role which they take on further helps to reduce mismatches between SMT policies and classroom practice.

Highdale's assistant head/head of department structure assumes that strategies for departmental development will be actively promoted by the assistant heads. This seems to have happened. A number of other consequences also seem to have flowed from this restructuring. Heads of department had had to become much more explicit about their planning processes than previously and, because of the assistant heads' teaching loads, many of the administrative and clerical tasks typically undertaken by deputy heads had had to be devolved to support staff. Such displacements were in line with North's view that 'teachers are for teaching'. Efforts had additionally been made to secure greater physical proximity of teaching rooms to encourage team work and collaborative planning.

Teachers generally saw the 'new' SMT structure as one of the signi-ficant changes of recent years and commended the 'flatter hierarchy' it embodied and the improved communication which arose from it. How-ever, there were some downsides. Staff referred to a (brief) period during the mid-1990s when one of the assistant heads had had difficulties with the demands of the role; a considerable amount revolved around their leadership and things could go badly wrong when post-holders were not up to the job. Their work-loads were also heavy. One head of department told us:

> the pressures are enormous because of the pressure to do each job well – as teacher, head of department and assistant head. Early on it was a 'headless chicken' job. It works better now because of some changes in job descriptions.

Some teachers also regretted the lack of a single person in the SMT directly responsible for discipline as incorporated in the previous system. Individual members of the SMT were aware of some of these difficulties but, having pushed for the changes and got them, they were not un-surprisingly committed to them.

Integrating the pastoral and the academic

Highdale's pastoral arrangements stretched back to the time when the school had been a secondary modern. North had made changing it a priority. The new structure, which was firmly in place by 1990, was based around 'vertical' tutor groups composed of around 25 pupils aged between 11 and 16, with each group being part of a house system. Pupils remain in the same tutor groups for their five years in the school, during which time the intention is that they should have the same tutor. The tutor was seen as the linchpin of the system, receiving and acting upon information from subject teachers, helping pupils to set personal targets and acting as the first point of contact with parents.

North was as committed to this reform as to that of the SMT. He had told colleagues that his personal philosophy was that

there are only three indicators [of success] to strive for and the greatest, in my opinion, is that each and every child should enjoy a relationship of trust with at least one member of staff.

The tutor role was seen as a challenging one which could impose heavy demands on teachers. One told us:

It is good to get to know tutees but writing everything down is a pain. . . . more is done to help the child now but no extra time is given to it – no work has been taken away to make room for the tutorial-related work.

Another teacher complained about the paperwork as well but added that 'there was no point in wasting energy fighting something you can't do anything about!'. More recently, Ofsted inspectors had commented on the 'problem of consistency of practice' across the various tutors involved; a series of activities had been planned with staff as a direct result.

The press for achievement

It should, perhaps, be stressed that neither of these two schools neg-lected the various devices others had employed to raise achievement. The monitoring of examination achievement at 16+ had become a grow-ing preoccupation at Highdale since 1990. The LEA had been at the 'leading edge' of value-added developments and Purchiss had been an enthusiastic participant in their initiatives. As a result the SMT had had a steady flow of information about the school's performance as well as that of individual departments. One outcome had been the identification of 'under-achieving' departments which had been required to set specific examination targets. Boys' under-achievement had also become a priority.

The effectiveness of monitoring is ultimately determined by the quality of the available data on pupils and the consistency with which tutors carry out their roles (as producers, disseminators, collators and interpreters of pupil data). Over the years the SMT had tried to tighten up and review these procedures, producing in the process a tutor's handbook and induction procedures for new tutors. More work in these areas was, however, still felt to be necessary.

Other (already familiar) strategies were also tried. For three years 'borderline' pupils had been targeted. Their tutors were asked to give them appropriate guidance and support. Initially, members of the SMT had tried to mentor small numbers of pupils from this group on a regular basis but, after a year, this experiment had collapsed under the weight of the SMT's work schedules and the lack of detailed planning which had gone into the scheme. Individual teachers had also put on extra classes for Year 11 pupils in lunch-breaks and after school.

Rowland teachers had developed a similar range of strategies. They, too, had focused on 'borderline' pupils at GCSE, chasing up homework and offering individual counselling. A review of the exam boards being used had been undertaken and all subject handbooks had been rewritten. The use of exemplar materials, which showed pupils what securing different grades in different subjects actually entailed, had been introduced (and was on display in the Learning Centre).

Like Highdale, the school had focused at a relatively early stage on improving pupils' basic skills. In Rowland's case this had involved the concentrated use of Successmaker with the 'bottom half' of the Year 7 entry. Highdale, meanwhile, had introduced a paired reading scheme into Year 7 tutor time, involving older pupils listening to weak readers for ten minutes a day.

The leadership of change

The leadership of change at Rowland was undertaken on several fronts in fairly rapid succession. The scale of the changes to middle management was considerable but had passed off with only minor 'resistance'. The encouragement to focus on changes in the learning and curricular areas had begun to become a consistent message. The philosophy of the Rowland pupil had been developed; this included an interest in their rights and responsibilities as well as getting the best out of each of them in both academic and affective terms. And, notwithstanding the nature and extent of the changes which had been put in place, some intellectual and emotional 'openness' within the school had been retained. In the process South had succeeded not only in taking the school apart, with a view to minimizing barriers to change, but also in putting it together again. It was a bold strategy, but one which seemed to have paid off.

There were two distinct phases to the change process at Highdale. The period 1988–90 was one of new ideas and the laying of foundations for new structures. Since that time implementation and consolidation had continued. The latter phase was accompanied by a steady improvement in exam performances as well. It is interesting, however, that the head, reflecting on the changes, said that there had been 'no grand plan, things just evolved'. This may, however, have been somewhat disingenuous. A lot of the post-1990 changes did 'evolve' but from a 'platform' whose foundations were already in place. Although causal links between these developments and improved performance cannot be definitively established, there is a persuasive prima-facie case for saying that the climate of careful and considered development had had beneficial effects.

For many staff Sam Purchiss had progressively emerged as the key innovator – the 'mind behind the key changes' and those which had subsequently followed. Although North was perhaps a more 'invisible' figure, his influence was none the less pervasive. He described himself as a 'benevolent dictator'. Their sharing of the leadership roles was similar, in *some* respects, to that of Randall and Drake at Compton. Separating out their respective contributions is consequently not easy.

The 'platform for change' consisted of two substantial innovations – the assistant head/head of department structure and the house system. The first arose primarily from Purchiss's thinking and that of other sympathetic heads of department. The vital insight which they sought to realize was that 'the school in general, but the SMT in particular, are seen to be publicly committed to the importance of learning and teaching and, by implication, committed to the importance of the classroom practitioner'. Crucially, however, the head supported and encouraged this thinking, biding his time until he was able to make the new assistant head appointments to form the core of the SMT. The house/tutor system, on the other hand, was North's 'brain-child', based on his central belief that individual pupils should have 'someone they can turn to'. In tandem the two principles provided a succinct and straightforward 'philosophy' which could be shared with staff.

Conclusions

One lesson both schools had learnt was that major changes, once implemented, have to be maintained as original enthusiasms wane, staff leave, new appointments are made and other concerns fight for prominence on the agenda. Another lesson was that innovation can result in substantial work-loads, not merely for the original instigators but also for those who take on their implications. Change can also generate both opposition and nostalgia. Neither school was alone in having to face up to these challenges, but to sustain their positions both had to find ways of living with them.

The evidence from these two cases suggests that both had succeeded in focusing their change agendas on to two or three issues. In each a concern to restructure the organization seems to have gone hand-in-hand with an increasing commitment to making a difference at the learning level. In their quest for strategies to enhance pupils' learning, what seems to have marked these schools out was their determination that reform efforts should be judged, largely but not exclusively, in terms of their impact on classroom practices. A central feature of the experiences of these schools was the extent to which their improvement efforts had focused on teaching and learning. In both there was a determination on the part of the leadership to place learning at the centre. This appears to have been done both at the level of structure (in the schools' development plans) and at the level of culture (with teachers being encouraged to talk about teaching).

Talking about teaching took a number of different forms. It included discussing strategies for instruction as well as expectations in relation to student learning. At the same time discussions of teaching were buttressed by changes to the schools' organization; new structural arrangements were put in place specifically to support changes in teaching.

All these changes were deliberately introduced in addition to the more familiar responses seen in the previous two chapters. Both Rowland and Highdale were unusual in their understanding of the need to take the medium-term view. In neither case was organizational restructuring an end in itself.

Taken together, the schools studied in these four chapters provide evidence of different improvement trajectories. In combination they can be considered as describing successive stages of a hypothetical development sequence through which a school might progress from being initially ineffective to becoming effective and improving. Whether an initially ineffective school could move rapidly through the levels, or perhaps even 'jump' an intermediate one, is unclear. The two schools in the present chapter were already at a level of effectiveness to which Park and Compton were only aspiring. As a result much of the 'common curriculum' of school improvement could already be assumed to be in place, enabling both Highdale and Rowland to tackle seriously the issue of enhancing classroom teaching and learning. The experience of Haystock is, however, also interesting in this respect and suggests that a higher-level concern with improving teaching and learning may emerge sooner rather than later. Whether such trajectories are invariant is a question to which we return in our final chapter.

Notes

1 Curriculum Plus was a school-wide project aimed at curriculum enhancement.
2 Successmaker is a computer package designed to give pupils structured experiences of, and practice in, the basic skills of literacy and numeracy.

▶ ▶ ▷ **Part III**

PATTERNS OF CHANGE?

▶ ▶ ▷ **9**

STARTING-POINTS AND PATTERNS OF CHANGE

The first half of the 1990s was a period of considerable change in the 12 secondary schools we studied. All of them were committed, to a greater or lesser extent, to school improvement. Among them, however, there were sizeable differences in what each school judged 'school improvement' to be, where they chose to place their energies and what they believed they had achieved.

A very considerable number of changes were reported to us during the course of our visits to schools. The first stage of our analysis, therefore, was to try to find some broad areas where it was clear that at least some of the schools we were studying had initiated (or experienced) changes. Our initial list of possible activities extended to some 80 items, which we felt to be too many to handle. On the other hand, as we reduced the numbers of categories, we were aware that meanings could become confounded. Eventually, and after some experimentation, we settled on building up 19 areas from the data.[1]

The next stage was for the two members of our team most familiar with each school to make a series of summary judgements about the extent of change which had occurred in each of these areas over the last five years. For a school to have changed their approach to a particular area over the last five years should not, of course, be confused with their improving it. A 'low' score could mean either that the school was already functioning well in this area, or that it had attempted to change some aspect of its practice but had not got very far, or some combination of the two.[2]

For the purpose of this discussion we have grouped the 19 areas under three broad headings relating to changes in the schools in terms of their mission and ethos, focus on achievement and approaches to planning and management. The allocation of particular areas to one or other of these three broad approaches is, of course, a heuristic device. We leave the question of how particular approaches might have been linked together in practice to a later stage.

Common areas for change

There were some areas in which the majority of schools in the sample were engaged in change (see Table 9.1, column 2). In the general area of mission and ethos, for example, three-quarters of the schools seem to have given considerable attention to the nature of their 'activities with parents' and produced what we judged to be 'a lot of change'.[3] More time had been spent interacting with parents and seeking their views; more attention had been given to what home–school partnerships were expected to produce; and moribund parent–teacher associations had been injected with a fresh sense of energy.

Just over half the schools (seven) had changed the ways in which they handled 'rewards, recognition and sanctions' for pupils. They had emphasized the importance of good pupil behaviour, enforced their attendance policies, celebrated success at awards evenings and, perhaps, introduced or re-introduced a school uniform.

Just over half the schools (seven) were judged to have undertaken 'a lot of change' in relation to the strategies they employed for 'maximizing exam grades'. To improve pupils' performances the schools had adopted such tactics as entering the majority of pupils for more examinations and paying particular attention to 'borderline' candidates. At the same time more attention was given to monitoring departmental exam results and their choice of exam boards and syllabuses. Many of the schools had set up strategies for pupil monitoring and some were engaging in more formalized target-setting. Many had initiated mentoring programmes which offered regular support to designated pupils. In several of the schools extra classes (beyond those timetabled) were being provided for older pupils in lunch-time and twilight slots as well as during the Easter break.

Another area in which the schools had stepped up activities was in relation to their 'policies for teaching and learning'. Half the schools were judged to have undergone 'a lot of change' in this area. Time had been spent producing or refining codes of classroom conduct whose purpose was to secure a firmer foundation for behaviour and discipline; staff working parties had developed procedures which commanded widespread support; and greater attention had been given to homework policies and practices across different departments.

Finally, there were several common changes in the area of planning and management. Three-quarters of the schools had changed the 'management

Table 9.1   The nature and extent of changes over five years in the
12 schools

Area of change	Mean change*	No. of schools where 'a lot of change' took place**
Mission and ethos		
Nature of school mission	1.3	5
Rewards, recognition and sanctions for pupils	1.6	7
Responsibilities given to pupils	1.4	5
Involvement of parents in school's activities	1.7	9
Building of relationships with external group (feeder schools, industry, local media, etc.)	1.4	4
Appearance of school environment	1.3	4
Focus on achievement		
Strategies for maximizing exam grades	1.3	7
Structure and content of curriculum (timetable, length of day, etc.)	1.2	3
Provision of extra-curricular activities	0.9	1
Policies for teaching and learning (codes of conduct, homework, etc.)	1.5	6
Learning environment and resources	1.3	4
Processes of teaching and learning (classroom management, teaching methods, etc.)	1.1	3
Planning and management		
Management style of the SMT	1.7	9
Structure of the SMT	1.7	7
Arrangements for consensual/participative management and planning	1.6	6
Development strategies for individual departments/faculties	1.2	3
Structure of middle management	1.0	5
Integration of academic and pastoral responsibilities	1.2	4
Involvement of external support (LEA, external projects, etc.)	1.3	6

* The extent of change over the past five years was judged on a four-point scale where
0 = 'little or no change'; 1 = 'some change'; 2 = 'a lot of change'; and 3 = 'an exceptional
amount of change'.
** Includes schools where an 'exceptional amount of change' took place.

style' of the SMT. Management teams saw themselves as having made
strenuous efforts to become more 'democratic' and more 'participative'.
They had also been concerned to become more 'visible'; nearly all of
them reported that they engaged in 'management by walking about'.

Staff often perceived changes of management style to have coincided with changes in leadership. Certainly, at such stages in a school's history, it was easier for participants to observe and understand what had been happening. However, we also found considerable evidence that other changes in the SMT could be just as important. In particular, while the recruitment of 'fresh blood' to a school was frequently referred to as *the* catalyst for change, we ourselves were surprised by the number of occasions on which it turned out (at least in the schools we were studying) that the impetus had emerged from *within* the school. At Rowland, for example, the decision to promote the deputy (who had already initiated a number of changes) to the position of headteacher sent out clear signals to the staff about what could be expected, and at Compton it was again the effects of an internal promotion which provided the main spur.

Changes in management style were frequently accompanied by other reforms to management arrangements intended to signal and reinforce changes in schools' direction. Prominent among these was some restructuring of 'the roles of senior management' (the number of positions and the responsibilities of those involved), which occurred in seven of the 12 schools. Behind such reforms was a concern to 'flatten the hierarchy' and increase communication with departmental heads and classroom teachers. Indeed, in a small number of cases, redefined teaching roles for members of the SMT had been introduced.

Changes to the formal structures of school management can signal that reform is on the agenda but they are unlikely, by themselves, to be sufficient. What seemed to determine the success or otherwise of such changes was the extent to which staff felt more 'consensual and participative approaches' to management and planning had been introduced. Significant changes in the ways planning and related activities were undertaken were found in half the schools, with much greater use, for example, of working parties and task forces than previously. There was also greater emphasis on shared codes of procedure ('the way we do things round here'), some of which had become incorporated into staff planners and handbooks. However, while the majority of schools had *attempted* to change their practices, they had clearly met with varying degrees of success.

Many of the changes schools undertook were related to each other (tables not shown). Schools which were judged to have changed their strategies for maximizing exam grades were also likely to have initiated changes in their policies for teaching and learning, given some attention to their learning environment and resources and made changes to the schools' physical appearance.[4] There again, schools which had emphasized rewards, recognition and sanctions for pupils were likely to have spent time on their strategies for maximizing exam grades, on their policies for teaching and learning, on the processes of teaching and learning and strategies for individual departments.

In short, if schools initiated certain kinds of changes they tended to initiate others, although whether there were any coherent patterns remains to be seen. There was one particularly interesting exception, however, to this general pattern. Changes in the structure and style of SMTs, along with moves towards more consensual and participative approaches to planning and management, were not related to any of the other changes schools were judged to have undertaken.[5]

Less common areas for change

It is clear that there were some areas where the majority of schools felt the need to act. Some of the other areas listed in Table 9.1, however, were ones where we judged only small numbers of schools to have changed. For example, the majority had simply been circumspect in engaging *directly* in activities whose principal focus was on the 'processes of classroom teaching and learning'.[6] When they did get round to such concerns the strategies they adopted were fairly constrained: school-wide discussions of teaching and learning, the identification of models of good practice, the arrangement of whole-school in-service sessions and general expressions of interest in facilitating better teaching and learning. Furthermore, there was frequently a diffidence verging on a reluctance to go further down this route.

In three of the schools rather more was happening. These schools were trying, in different but related ways, to raise questions about what affected pupils' classroom experiences. They were doing such things as: encouraging classroom observation by colleagues, heads of department or the SMT, followed by discussions among those involved; appraisals of classroom management and pedagogic skills; the encouragement of an enquiry orientation to teaching and learning; and the fostering of collaborative or team approaches to teaching as a means of sharing good practice. It was clear, however, that relatively few of the schools we studied had begun to address issues of teaching and learning, at least as they impinged on pupils' classroom experiences, in any very systematic way.

The schools which did engage with the processes of teaching and learning did so in tandem with a number of other changes (tables not shown). The correlational data indicate that they were likely to have used strategies to maximize exam grades, given attention to their policies for teaching and learning, improved their learning resources and environment, changed aspects of the rewards, recognition and sanctions for pupils and made efforts to integrate their pastoral and academic structures.

There were several other areas where changes in schools' approaches were modest. There was agreement, for example, in most of the schools, that what went on within subject departments was central. However, we judged only three schools in the sample to have changed the ways they were working 'a lot' by having 'development strategies' for individual departments (see Table 9.1). There was widespread awareness among the SMT's of the extent to which departments differed in their interest in (and commitment to) change. But the majority of SMTs were fairly circumspect about intervening at this level. Most had started off assuming that most members of staff would be caught up (somehow or other) in school-wide initiatives. Subsequently many of them had had to come to terms with the extent to which such optimistic assumptions were being not merely *not* sustained but, on occasion, expressly challenged. In only a couple of schools, however, was the resistance overt; more often it was simply a case of inertia.

Management teams varied in the ways in which they tried to handle departmental-level issues. Mostly they pinned their hopes on changes of key personnel but these, of course, could only rarely be planned for. In three schools, however, there were clear signs that departmental development strategies were being tried out. Members of the SMT would take specific responsibility for the 'low performance' of particular departments and try to find ways forward. A metaphor coined to describe what was going on was that of 'coaching'. Some interest was also expressed in securing external support for these departments. However, many of the SMTs retained rather pessimistic views about what it was possible and appropriate to do at departmental level.

Schools which had developed strategies for departments were likely to have given attention to rewards, recognition and sanctions for pupils and, albeit to a considerably lesser extent, the processes of teaching and learning. They also seem to have been prepared to change the ways their middle managements were structured and to have been more willing to change their 'overall curriculum structures' by redesigning the timetable and extending the school day (tables not shown).

In sum, while there were some areas where the greater majority of schools had initiated changes over the last five years, only a small minority seem to have been engaged in changes connected with the processes of teaching and learning at classroom level. The number which had embarked on development strategies for individual departments was equally small.

The experience of change

Up to this point we have concentrated on some of the specific changes which occurred across the schools. Table 9.2 provides some indication of the extent of change experienced in each of the schools in relation to the 19 areas on which the research team made judgements. Across the

Table 9.2   Patterns of change across the 19 areas, broken down by school

School	Extent of change over last five years		
	Little or no change	*Some change*	*A lot of change**
Rowland	1	4	14
Blackstone	2	7	10
Compton	1	9	9
Park	0	5	14
Highdale	0	11	8
Keystone	0	9	10
Aldley	1	6	12
Canonbury	6	10	3
Palmerton	4	10	5
Haystock	3	9	7
Foxton	9	9	1
Burdland	2	12	5

* See Table 9.1 for definitions.

sample as a whole there was clearly considerable change. The table suggests, however, that the extent of change varied considerably across the schools. Rowland and Park, for example, were judged to have experienced 'a lot of change' in no fewer than 14 of the areas; indeed virtually every area of these two schools was judged to have changed to some extent over the past five years. By contrast, Foxton and Canonbury only experienced 'a lot of change' in a few areas; they were judged to have had 'little or no change' in nine and six areas, respectively.

The extent of differences between schools is borne out by teachers' reports of the extent of change. We asked those we interviewed to make judgements about how much change had occurred in their schools over the last five years (see Table 9.3). They were most likely to report changes in the area of management and planning. In the median schools around 60 per cent of the teachers reported 'substantial' changes in the 'ways the school was run and organized' and around 50 per cent reported similar levels of change with respect to the school's 'attitude and approach to planning'. Somewhere over 40 per cent also indicated that their school's 'curriculum organization and delivery' had changed 'substantially' over the same period.

Changes in the area of the school's 'ethos, culture or climate' were less frequently reported. Only around 30 per cent of the teachers in the median school suggested that the changes had been 'substantial'. Finally, in the area of the 'quality of teaching and learning' the changes were lower still. In the median school well under 20 per cent felt that the

Table 9.3 Teachers' reports of the extent of 'substantial' change
in their school over the last five years

Area of change*	Percentage of teachers in the school reporting 'substantial' amounts of change over the last 5 years		
	Highest % in a school	Median %s in a school**	Lowest % in a school
Ways the school is run and organized	100	65 59	14
The ethos, culture or climate of the school	80	35 27	13
School's attitude and approach to planning	93	50 50	4
School's curriculum organization and delivery	71	46 43	4
Quality of teaching and learning in the school	60	17 17	4

* Respondents were given the opportunity to select one of three alternatives in relation to each area of change – 'substantial amount of change', 'moderate' or 'very little' – as well as to comment on the direction of changes. The percentages refer to the proportion of staff interviewed in each school who reported that the changes had been 'substantial' and in the general direction of improvement.
** With 12 schools the median falls between the percentages for two schools.

changes had been 'substantial'. Teachers may not, of course, have been as aware of changes in this latter area outside their own particular subjects as some of the school-wide developments referred to above. None the less, its position some way behind the others needs to be noted.

The evidence from Table 9.3 confirms that there was very considerable variation in the extent to which changes were experienced in the different areas across the schools. In one school the entire staff felt that the changes to the ways the school was run and organized had been 'substantial'; in another only 14 per cent did so. In one school 60 per cent of the staff reported 'substantial' changes to the quality of teaching and learning; in another only 4 per cent did so.

Figure 9.1 shows the extent to which these various changes occurred separately or together across the 12 individual schools and permits some conjectures about the extent of 'clustering' across different areas. For example, changes in four of the five areas at Rowland were clustered together, with between half and three-quarters of the staff reporting 'substantial' changes over the last five years. There was a similar 'clustering' at Canonbury where four of the five responses fell between 10 per cent and 20 per cent. However, there were also several cases where the

School	0%	10%	20%	30%	40%	50%	60%	70%	80%	90%
Rowland					Ethos	Planning	T&L Organization	Curr.Org.		
Blackstone				T&L	Curr.Org.		Planning	Ethos	Organization	
Compton			T&L		Planning	Ethos Organization	Curr.Org.			
Park						T&L		Curr.Org.	Ethos	Planning Organization
Highdale			Ethos	Curr.Org.	T&L	Planning			Organization	
Keystone			Ethos T&L			Planning Curr.Org.	Organization			
Aldley				Ethos T&L		Planning Curr.Org.	Organization			
Canonbury	T&L	Ethos Planning	Organization Curr.Org.							
Palmerton			T&L		Ethos Curr.Org.	Planning	Organization			
Haystock			T&L		Curr.Org.			Ethos	Organization Planning	
Foxton		Ethos T&L				Planning Curr.Org.	Organization			
Burdland		T&L	Ethos			Curr.Org.		Planning Organization		

Figure 9.1 Percentages of teachers in the 12 schools reporting 'substantial' changes over the last five years

Table 9.4 Correlations between perceived changes in the 12 schools

	Organization	Ethos	Planning	Curriculum organization
Ethos	0.58	–		
Planning	0.62	0.21	–	
Curriculum organization	0.15	0.00	0.60	–
Quality of teaching and learning	0.56	0.31	0.26	0.37

response clearly depended on the area. Over 80 per cent of the staff at Highdale, for example, felt that the school's organization had changed 'substantially' but only over 10 per cent felt the ethos had. There was a very similar pattern at Burdland.

The underlying structure of these relationships is reported in Table 9.4. When, for example, teachers reported that there had been 'substantial' changes in the ways their school was run and organized, they were also quite likely to report changes in its ethos and attitude and approach to planning. Changes in a school's curriculum organization and delivery were also related to changes in its planning. Interestingly, however, while changes in the school's quality of teaching and learning were related to changes in the ways it was 'run and organized', they appeared to be only weakly related to changes in its ethos, planning and curriculum organization.

Change and 'resistance'

We have focused so far on what the schools in the sample did to *make* changes happen. In half of them, however, we noted 'sources of resistance'. In four of the schools we judged there to be 'some resistance' and in two 'quite a lot'. In the other six schools, however, resistance to change was, in our judgement, quite minimal.

In two schools the current size of the group of 'resisters' was said to be rather small yet quite influential. The deputy at Keystone referred to them in the following terms:

> There are some people who . . . I call them black paper writers. And we've one or two who are very very negative and we've got a few staff the head and I refer to as charge hands.

Although there was possibly an ideological dimension to 'resistance' in this case, low morale was also a prominent factor. A head of department at Palmerton also referred to the existence of such a group:

> The headteacher set out his vision early on but a vocal minority seems to dominate . . . it needs a more forceful drive to take us further.

Elsewhere the sources of inertia were seen to have grown as the staff themselves got older. A teacher at Canonbury said:

> I'm going to say that we've got a very old staff, a lot of them are very close to retirement and do not want to take on yet another initiative.

Indeed, a similar analysis was offered by a deputy in the same school. Seeking to explain why initiatives had failed to take off in the school, he commented:

> The staff? They came, they stayed, they're ageing, they're tiring.

'Resistance' was negatively correlated with some of the 19 change areas but, interestingly, not with others. Schools where there was more 'resistance' were a good deal less likely to have initiated changes in their policies for teaching and learning, their processes of teaching and learning, their strategies for maximizing exam grades, their rewards, recognition and sanctions for pupils, the responsibilities given to pupils and their development strategies for individual departments (table not shown).

Teachers in schools where there was such 'resistance' were particularly likely to report that there had been 'little or no change' in the 'quality of teaching and learning' over the last five years. They were also more likely to say that there had been 'little or no change' in their school's curriculum organization and delivery, in its ethos, culture or climate and in the ways it was run and organized (table not shown).

Concluding comments

There were some common features to the change processes across the schools. A sizeable proportion of them had changed their management styles over the last five years and taken steps to secure greater parental involvement. The greater majority had not made 'substantial' changes to the processes of teaching and learning and hardly any at all had changed the provision of extra-curricular activities. With respect to many of the other changes, however, the schools were more evenly divided; some had embarked on changes, others had not.

Teachers, for their part, confirmed many of these assessments. They were more likely to report changes to the ways their schools were run and organized and their ethos or culture than to the quality of teaching and learning. Schools where we noted more 'resistance' were a good deal less likely to have introduced changes in the areas of teaching and learning.

Individual readers will differ in the extent to which they attribute importance to these various changes. In the following chapter we explore the extent to which they were systematically related to one particular dimension, namely changes in the schools' effectiveness over time.

Notes

1 Most 'areas' were composed of sub-items which were offered as 'exemplars' during the coding stages. Preliminary descriptions of each of the areas were drawn up on a pilot basis and then refined in the light of team members' experiences of trying to make judgements. The number of sub-items which were judged to contribute to each area varied according to the area concerned.

2 The subjective nature of these judgements needs to be acknowledged. Obviously what was judged by those who knew one school well to amount to 'a lot of change' over the last five years might not have been perceived in the same light by another pair working in a different school. To increase the degree of comparability across the schools one member of the research team attempted to validate the various ratings given to each school in the light of the evidence available. This scrutiny of the judgements for each school resulted in some revisions to the final ratings (which form the basis for Table 9.1).

3 The contrast here is between those schools where 'a lot of change' took place and those where 'little or none' occurred. We are reasonably confident that other observers would confirm the differences between these two positions. Some of the other contrasts (between 'some' change and 'a lot of change', for example) may also be of interest but are not given prominence here.

4 Correlations of around 0.6 or above are of particular interest here.

5 Changes in the areas of parental activities, rewards and recognition for pupils, strategies for exam grades and policies for teaching and learning were all strongly related to changes in at least four other areas. By contrast, changes to the structure of the SMT and moves towards consensual planning and management were only related to one each, while changes in management style were not systematically related to any of the other 18 changes whatsoever.

6 There is further support for this position from the evidence relating to whether the schools had had a change of head during the last five years. The only area on which all new headteachers seem likely to have worked was in relation to their school's physical appearance.

10

SOME CORRELATES OF SCHOOL IMPROVEMENT

Were changes in some areas more important than others in contributing to school improvement over time? One simple way of addressing this question is to subject the measures of change explored in the previous chapter to statistical analysis. A series of analyses was therefore undertaken in which the relationships between schools' improvements in effectiveness were related to the 19 change measures.[1]

With only 12 cases available for statistical analysis some care is needed in interpreting the results. At best, the correlational patterns can be no more than suggestive of what seems to have worked. While each contains an implicit assumption about what might bring about changes in performance, correlations do not, of course, necessarily imply causal relationships. Furthermore, confirmatory work on larger samples would be desirable. None the less, some of the patterns which did emerge seemed particularly interesting.[2]

Some factors driving change?

The correlations between the various change measures discussed in the previous chapter and schools' 'improvements in effectiveness' are presented in Table 10.1. Four turned out to be strongly correlated with improvements.

The first of these was the extent to which the school had exploited various opportunities or 'tactics' for 'maximizing pupils' exam grades'. These included such things as increasing the numbers of exam subjects for which pupils were entered, identifying pupils at the 'borderline' for extra support and mentoring, providing additional revision classes and reviewing the choice of exam boards.

Table 10.1 Correlations between changes in effectiveness and extent of change in schools

Area of change*	Correlation with change in effectiveness**
Tactics for maximizing exam grades	0.64***
Policies for supporting teaching and learning	0.64
Processes of teaching and learning	0.60
Responsibilities given to pupils	0.65
Development strategies for individual departments	0.54
Rewards, recognition and sanctions for pupils	0.51
Involvement of parents	0.49
Management style of SMT	0.47
Integration of academic and pastoral responsibilities	0.44
Structure of middle management	0.40
Nature of school mission	0.38
Learning environment and resources	0.36
Provision of extra-curricular activities	0.36
Building external relationships with key groups	0.41
Structure and content of curriculum	0.30
School appearance	0.36
Consensual/participative management	0.31

* The areas of change are described more fully in Chapter 9.
** These were based on the estimates of improvements in schools' effectiveness described in Chapter 4.
*** With the sample sizes in Tables 10.1 and 10.2 a correlation of 0.40 is statistically significant at the 10% level with a one-tailed test; a correlation of 0.49 is statistically significant at the 5% level; and a correlation of 0.65 at the 1% level. Given the nature of the changes being explored, and the indications in the literature about their likely associations with change, one-tailed tests seem justified. The factors are listed in terms of the size of their correlations. However, it should be noted that these are indicative measures of the strength of the associations and should not be interpreted too precisely.

The second was the extent to which the school had developed 'policies for supporting teaching and learning', including the development of more coherent codes of conduct relating to pupil behaviour in class and increased use of homework.

The third was the extent to which the school had begun to tackle the 'processes of teaching and learning' at classroom level, including the use of classroom observation as part of the appraisal process, the fostering of collaborative work as a means of sharing good practice among teachers and the encouragement of discussion and an enquiry orientation towards teaching and learning.

The fourth was the extent to which 'responsibilities had been given to pupils', including the emphasis on providing support for pupils to manage the learning process themselves, the more active seeking and use of pupil views and the efforts made to involve pupils more prominently in the life of the school.

Several other change dimensions also turned out to be significantly correlated with 'improvements in schools' effectiveness' although not so strongly (see the block of items with 'middling' correlations in Table 10.1). These included: changes in the rewards, recognition and sanctions for pupils; the development of ways to involve parents; the extent to which the school had adopted development strategies for individual departments; the initiation of changes in the structure of middle management; and the greater integration of academic and pastoral responsibilities.

In a situation where schools were engaged in change on many fronts it is difficult to be confident that some dimensions of change were *necessarily* more important than others. None the less, it is of interest that the statistical analysis draws attention to the importance of both short-term tactics related to improving exam results and aspects of teaching and learning at the classroom level.

Teachers' reports of change

There is some additional support for the potential importance of the 'teaching and learning' dimensions from teachers' own reports of the changes that occurred in their schools. Each teacher we interviewed was asked to make a judgement about how much change had occurred in the last five years in relation to various aspects of their schools. There was a strong tendency for the schools which had higher proportions of teachers reporting that there had been 'substantial' changes in the 'quality of teaching and learning in their school' over the last five years to have improved more rapidly in terms of their effectiveness (see Table 10.2).

The correlations between 'rapid' improvement and teachers reporting 'substantial' changes in either 'the ethos, culture or climate' of their school or the 'ways the curriculum was organized and delivered' were less strong. Interestingly, in the two areas where teachers were most

Table 10.2 Correlations between changes in effectiveness and teachers' reports of the extent of 'substantial' changes in five areas

Area in which teachers in a school reported 'substantial' changes over last five years*	Correlation with change in effectiveness*
The quality of teaching and learning in the school	0.63
The ethos, culture or climate of the school	0.49
The school's curriculum, organization and delivery	0.45
The ways the school is run and organized	0.23
The school's attitude and approach to planning (weak negative correlation)	−0.26

* See Table 9.3 for further details of these items and Table 10.1 for information about levels of statistical significance.

likely to report that there had been 'substantial' changes in their schools, namely in the ways the school was run and organized and in its 'attitude and approach to planning', there was little or no relationship. Indeed, in the latter case, the relationship was actually negative, suggesting that a school which had needed (or decided) to concentrate its change efforts in this area during this period had probably missed the boat. The introduction of planning structures may be a necessary condition for change but does not seem to have been a sufficient one (see Louis and Miles 1992).

There was one other relationship which proved to be strongly related to schools' 'improvements in effectiveness'. The schools where members of the research team judged the 'sources of resistance' to be strongest turned out to be those which improved least (table not shown). With the benefit of hindsight, we might usefully have spent more time analysing this aspect of schools' functioning.

Connections to improvement?

It is clear that a number of different approaches seem to have been associated with more rapid improvement. But how were these related to each other? Table 10.3 presents a correlation matrix showing the relationships between the ten variables shown as having strong or middling correlations with improvement in Table 10.1.

Taking the first four variables listed in the table, it is evident that three of them were related to each other.[3] Schools which had given attention to their tactics for maximizing exam grades were very likely to have worked on their policies for teaching and learning as well ($r = 0.79$) and quite likely to have done something about the processes of teaching and learning ($r = 0.69$). There again, schools which had worked on their policies for teaching and learning were very likely to have worked on the processes of teaching and learning ($r = 0.82$). The structure of the correlations is highly suggestive of a series of connected approaches, and the additional correlations between these three approaches and the other seven listed in the table confirm this impression.

On the other hand, schools which had given more responsibilities to pupils (the fourth approach on the list) seem to have been distinctive. These schools had taken steps to enhance what was expected of pupils and the levels of responsibility they were asked to shoulder. They had actively sought out pupils' views, introduced or reinvigorated the school council, perhaps recruited some pupils as prefects or given them other responsibilities as well as giving pupils more prominent roles with respect to, for example, visitors to the school. This approach was only weakly correlated with the first three mentioned above (the correlations ranged between 0.16 and 0.36) and similarly weakly related to the other

Table 10.3 Correlations between ten approaches associated with improvement

	Strategies to maximize exam grades*	Policies for teaching and learning	Processes of teaching and learning	Responsibilities given to pupils	Departmental strategies	Rewards and sanctions for pupils	Parental involvement	SMT style	Academic/pastoral integration
Policies for teaching and learning*	**0.79**	–							
Processes of teaching and learning	**0.69**	**0.82**	–						
Responsibilities given to pupils	0.16	0.36	0.33	–					
Departmental strategies	**0.49**	0.23	**0.50**	0.27	–				
Rewards and sanctions for pupils	**0.60**	**0.66**	**0.72**	0.34	**0.75**	–			
Parental involvement	0.41	**0.70**	**0.52**	0.29	0.00	0.26	–		
SMT style	0.20	0.25	0.02	0.31	-0.04	0.05	0.23	–	
Academic/pastoral integration	**0.57**	**0.60**	**0.65**	-0.03	0.37	**0.52**	0.13	-0.06	–
Structure of middle management	0.27	0.10	0.41	0.21	**0.66**	0.45	-0.27	-0.31	**0.61**

Note: See Chapter 9 for fuller descriptions of the variables. Statistically significant correlations at the 5% level are in bold (see Tables 10.1 and 10.4).

Table 10.4   Correlations between four approaches associated with improvement and teachers' perceptions of change

	Organization*	Ethos	Planning	Quality of teaching and learning	Curriculum organization
Strategies to maximize exam grades*	−0.11	0.01	0.02	**0.57**	0.36
Policies for teaching and learning	0.31	0.32	0.32	**0.70**	0.47
Processes of teaching and learning	0.35	0.05	0.19	**0.78**	**0.49**
Responsibilities given to pupils	0.39	**0.74**	−0.11	0.36	0.37

* Fuller descriptions of these items are available in Chapter 9. Statistically significant correlations are in bold (see Table 10.1).

seven approaches listed in Table 10.3. Again it follows from the correlational structure that a school which combined this approach with one (or more) of the three listed above (relating respectively to tactics to maximize exam grades, policies for teaching and learning and the processes of teaching and learning) is likely to have made the most rapid progress.

Further support for the view that there may be 'alternative routes' to improvement can be seen in Table 10.4, which reports the correlations between the four approaches and teachers' perceptions of the changes in their schools over the last five years. Teachers in schools reporting that there had been 'substantial' changes in the quality of teaching and learning were very likely to be in schools which we judged to have given attention to the processes of teaching and learning ($r = 0.78$); they were quite likely to be in schools which had worked on their policies for teaching and learning ($r = 0.70$); and they were fairly likely to be in schools which had used various tactics to maximize their exam grades ($r = 0.57$). Again, however, the distinctiveness of the schools approaching improvement through the development of greater responsibilities for pupils is underlined by the correlational patterns. The only one of the five variables relating to teachers' perceptions to which this was related was that pertaining to changes in the school's ethos ($r = 0.74$); the correlation with perceived changes in the quality of teaching and learning was, by comparison, modest ($r = 0.36$).

Conclusions

Three tentative conclusions may be drawn from these analyses. First, 'rapid' improvement was linked to changes in the schools' use of various tactics for maximizing exam grades; their development of policies for supporting teaching and learning; the degree to which they had begun to tackle the processes of teaching and learning at classroom level; and the extent to which responsibilities had been given to pupils.

Second, schools which had improved more 'rapidly' had higher proportions of teachers reporting that there had been 'substantial' changes in the quality of teaching and learning over the last five years. In 'slowly' improving schools only a very small proportion of the staff (typically around one in ten or fewer) reported similar changes.

Third, there are some suggestions that while schools seem to have launched change initiatives on many fronts, their approaches to improvement could be bundled together. Schools which did some things also did others. The most rapidly improving schools seem, however, to have found ways of straddling distinctively different approaches at the same time.

Notes

1 For the purposes of this analysis schools were initially ordered in terms of the extent of their improvement over time (see Figure 4.2 for the outline framework). In order to create a more differentiated outcome measure, the schools were reassigned into five improvement groups instead of the original three. The first contained schools which were clearly improving 'rapidly' (that is, improving in their effectiveness over time), the next schools which were improving 'fairly rapidly', the third schools which were improving 'steadily' (remaining of average effectiveness over time), the fourth schools which were improving 'fairly steadily' and the fifth schools which were improving 'slowly' (declining in their effectiveness over time). A school which was initially of 'above average' effectiveness which was 'rapidly' improving headed these groupings; a school which was initially of 'below average' effectiveness and which was improving 'slowly' propped them up. While this measure was originally based on a sophisticated statistical analysis it is of interest that it was strongly correlated (0.74) with teachers' own perceptions of the extent to which there had been 'improvements in pupils' achievements' in their school over the last five years.

2 The dilemmas will be familiar to anyone who has attempted to combine quantitative and qualitative approaches. With the benefit of hindsight, we wish we had chosen larger samples on which to test the strength of the emerging evidence.

3 With a larger sample more sophisticated statistical analyses could be considered. In the present case we have preferred to keep things simple by confining our examination to the correlational structures.

11

BUILDING FOR IMPROVEMENT

The school improvement scene is changing. In the period between completing our fieldwork and turning to its interpretation a new government has come into office. Its predecessor had become increasingly interested in aspects of school improvement and had begun, albeit tentatively, to promote initiatives. A commitment to raising standards across schools, with parts of the programme embodied in legislation, is none the less a recent phenomenon. The explicit concern that 'intervention should be in inverse proportion to success' presents new challenges and, it must be said, new problems (DfEE 1997a).

It is easy to forget, as a result, that the expectation that most schools' performances would rise (more or less inexorably) from year to year is relatively new. Less than a decade ago anything more than the most marginal changes in schools' results would have been treated with suspicion. Attitudes began to change, however, with the implementation of the National Curriculum and the GCSE, and the introduction of league tables in the early 1990s provided a further 'jolt' to the system.

With hindsight, we can see that the national conditions within which 'school improvement' could take place were beginning to take hold. The idea that 'quite deliberate' efforts should be made to tackle the problem of 'poor' schools and 'make them better' can be traced back to the Plowden Report (Central Advisory Council for Education 1967). Plowden's vision, however, was cast in terms of absolute standards – the 'poor' schools were the ones attended by the educationally and socially disadvantaged.

It has taken the better part of three decades for this concern to return to the top of the policy agenda. As the Secretary of State put it in the White Paper: 'we must strive to eliminate, and never excuse, under-achievement in the most deprived parts of our country' (DfEE 1997a: 3). However, recast in the language of the popular press, the message has become translated into 'zero tolerance'. Within a relatively short period of time, schools have found the stakes escalating. Greater knowledge and understanding of how schools actually improve is at a premium.

When we come to review the progress schools have been making in recent years, we would do well to remember when the climate began to change. Up to the early 1990s a school could improve to some extent merely by running with and responding to the 'logics' of various national developments (the National Curriculum, the GCSE and league tables). While most of these involved modest rethinking of current practices, some progress (and certainly enough to assuage most potential critics) could be made without engaging very much at all in further changes to what was going on *within* the school. It was not until the mid-1990s that the majority of schools had to begin to face up to the real challenges of school improvement and the realization that they were in for the long haul. The pressures began to be reflected in the year-on-year rates of change – they quickly halved. It is at this point that the experiences of some of the schools we studied become of particular interest.

Defining 'improvement'

'Improvement' is an elusive term. In many studies its precise meaning is left implicit. After reviewing various alternatives we opted for a definition which combined elements of both the school effectiveness and school improvement research traditions. As has been common in most previous British studies, we used exam results as our measure of performance but took particular steps to ensure that what we were focusing on was (as far as we could make it) the contribution made by the school to its pupils' progress. An 'improving' school in our study, therefore, was one which 'increased in its effectiveness' over time. In other words, the amounts of 'value-added' it generated rose for successive cohorts of pupils.

Adopting this definition had implications for the typology of schools we subsequently developed. Schools were located in two dimensions: in terms of their initial effectiveness (which was estimated from the data we had available on the performance of their first cohort of pupils) and their improvement trajectory (which was based on their performance with subsequent cohorts). Combining the two dimensions produced a nine-category framework of schools ('above average' effectiveness and improving 'rapidly', 'above average' effectiveness and improving 'steadily' and so on through to 'below average' effectiveness and improving 'slowly') – see Figure 4.2.

Estimates of change and improvement

We were particularly interested in the question of how far schools could change in their *levels* of 'effectiveness' over time. The answer depends on knowing two things: the distance between the different levels; and schools' *rates* of improvement.

Multi-level analyses indicated that around 80 per cent of the differences in pupils' performances potentially attributable to schools were associated with the effectiveness dimension, leaving around 20 per cent associated with the improvement dimension. In other words, most schools which were identified as more effective in the first year continued to be more effective in subsequent years. Conversely, most schools which were identified as less effective in the first year continued to be less effective in subsequent years. Differences between schools in their effectiveness simply swamped any changes in effectiveness (upwards or downwards).

During the time-frames we employed between one in four and one in five schools were clearly changing in terms of performance; of this group, about half were improving and a roughly similar proportion deteriorating. In short, schools which are really changing in terms of their effectiveness are in rather short supply.

Our analyses also established schools' rates of improvement. A 'rapidly improving' school seems to have been increasing its exam scores by an average of around one grade in one subject per pupil per year. In comparison with some of the claims made in the educational press, such progress may seem comparatively modest. On the other hand, figures of this magnitude square with much of what we saw in the schools we studied. Furthermore, we concluded that three (or possibly four) years of such continuous improvement represented a 'good run'. For a school to change its 'label', however, by moving from one level of effectiveness to another (from, for example, being of 'below average' effectiveness to 'average' effectiveness) represented a considerable challenge. None of the schools in our study quite succeeded in making it definitively from one level to the next.

Given what we now know, prevailing notions of schools' 'naturally occurring' improvement trajectories strike us as quite simplistic (Gray and Wilcox 1995). Unfortunately lack of knowledge of a school's 'trajectory' creates the risk not merely of poor diagnosis but of inappropriate treatment.

Some problems in understanding change

The definition of a 'period of change' is, to some extent, arbitrary. Most of the staff we interviewed could point to a time or a series of events from which 'improvement' began to develop (the appointment of a new head being the most obvious form of demarcation). None the less, because of the particular mixes of external and internal factors operating in any particular school, each of them felt their starting-point was unique.

We attempted to tap into the 'natural histories' of different schools over roughly a five-year period (the last five years). This period did not always quite match those which teachers recalled; memories and events do not, of course, map neatly on to time-frames. None the less, we gained a number of insights into teachers' experiences of the change process. Few schools seemed to be making progress in a steady step-by-step manner. There were periods when things were reported to have changed fairly rapidly followed by periods of what might be termed 'consolidation'.

Leadership of major change initiatives was usually provided by the headteachers. Indeed, there seemed to be an assumption among many staff that a new head would bring in a (limited) programme of change; as a result, some teachers began to make preparations for the 'new' regime in advance of its arrival. Furthermore, where there was a recognition that the school had experienced significant problems in the past there was nearly always a clear expectation that the new management would do something about them. Even if there was no explicit mandate for change there was often an implicit one. One of the interesting findings to emerge from our case studies, however, was the frequency with which another member of the SMT took on a significant element of the 'leading improvement' role.

The challenge for 'reforming' heads, then, is to understand how rapidly they can move into action. However, judging a school's 'culture' is not necessarily straightforward (Hargreaves 1995; Hopkins and Harris 1997). Staff opinions can be all too readily divided into those who demonize previous heads (and the 'regimes' associated with them) and those who look back with nostalgia. We found that a particularly common form of such nostalgia was the celebration of the 'mythic deputy', often recalled as combining good relationships with colleagues with a firm, no-nonsense approach to discipline. When taking the temperature, new managements would do well to remember that such perceptions can cloud views about what needs to be done.

Although we selected schools on the basis that they were on different improvement trajectories and were progressing at different rates, almost all the institutions we studied in depth *claimed* to be 'improving' schools. In nearly every case their 'headline' exam statistics were better than a few years previously. Furthermore, as we noted in an earlier chapter, in all but one of the schools a high proportion of staff reported that there had been 'substantial' changes over the last five years in at least one of four areas (organization, planning, ethos or climate, and curriculum organization) and quite frequently in several of them. Most schools, in short, either had a 'success story' to tell or felt they could create one.

There were a number of ways in which they could legitimately do so. Only with respect to changes in the 'quality of teaching and learning' were the responses more muted.

Launching into improvement

There were few signs that the schools in our study engaged in lengthy analyses of their situations prior to launching into change programmes. Such programmes were often inaugurated by the production of a few 'sound-bite' rallying calls reflecting key beliefs of the heads and/or their SMTs. The question of whether these really constituted a 'programme' was only subsequently addressed. Initiatives were chosen from a wide range of options. However, although aims were often revised early on, we found little evidence of active attempts to embed them in the consciousness of staff and, still less, of pupils. Most of the schools in the sample achieved their goals not by following a closely worked-out plan or blueprint but by intuitively selecting what seemed the most appropriate actions at the time. The preferred approach was simply to launch one or two initiatives to 'set the ball rolling' and then to allow others to be set up in their wake. Without a coherent framework to plan developments, the number of such initiatives could expand quite rapidly.

Subsequently, and not altogether surprisingly, most schools discovered that there was more to sustaining change than they had originally envisaged. Most did their best and, to some extent, muddled through. They did not generally appear to have brought together individual initiatives (and the traditions they reflected) into coherent rationales capable of being internalized and, in time, institutionalized. They tried to plan, sometimes found themselves doing too much and then became aware of possible disjunctures between what was happening at whole-school level and in departments and classrooms. Interestingly, many of the teachers we talked to felt that their school was very much 'alone' in the choices it had made.

Areas of change and correlates of improvement

The individual initiatives which made up schools' change programmes were broadly similar from institution to institution, effectively amounting to something approaching a 'common curriculum' for school improvement. They could be grouped under the following more general themes:

• efforts to raise pupils' exam performances through such strategies as entering pupils for more exams and mentoring 'borderline' pupils;

- modifications to management structures and planning procedures to achieve greater staff (and to a lesser extent) pupil participation;
- attempts to change the school's culture or ethos;
- efforts to implement more coherent policies for teaching and learning in such areas as codes of classroom conduct and homework;
- changes to the ways in which the curriculum was organized, mostly in response to national reforms;
- refurbishment of the school environment and facilities;
- efforts to involve parents in their children's education and the community in the life of the school;
- more active marketing of the school; and
- giving attention to the processes of teaching and learning, including such things as fostering more discussion of classroom practices.

Many of the schools in our study tackled the first of the areas on this list, namely efforts to raise exam results directly. It is an interesting feature of the English approach to assessment at the end of compulsory schooling that it 'rewards' this kind of approach. Many also worked on their policies for supporting teaching and learning. Only a small minority, however, had engaged in activities in relation to supporting classroom processes of teaching and learning. As our subsequent analyses indicated, the most rapidly improving schools had probably found ways of doing all three of these things. They had managed to focus directly on aspects of pupils' achievement, organizational policies supporting teaching along with aspects of classroom culture and practice at much the same time.

The influence of departments

In most of the schools we studied there was substantial variation between different subject departments in terms of performance and general attitudes to change. The range of responses we encountered among middle management was also considerable. They ranged from the 'young Turks' at one extreme to the (usually but not invariably) older 'resisters' at the other.

Schools' strategies for departmental development were relatively embryonic around the time we were studying them. The main influences for change at this level were perceived as: the head of department; the National Curriculum; and the choices to be made between different exam boards and syllabuses. Referring to specific lessons which we had observed, teachers usually identified departments' schemes of work and, more occasionally, their departments' development plans as the principal influences on what they did rather than any school-wide initiatives (cf. Sammons *et al.* 1997). Some effects were attributed to involvement in external projects and interventions by LEA advisory staff, although in both cases such mentions were considerably less frequent.

Underlying school-wide initiatives were a number of often optimistic assumptions about how departments would be affected. In general, we judged departmental strategies for change to be only 'loosely coupled' to school-wide strategies. It was an unusual school which had secured coherence.

Effects of change on teachers and pupils

Most of the change programmes the schools in our sample initiated involved forms of 'work intensification' for teachers. In allowing a dozen (or more) separate initiatives to bloom they had, in their enthusiasm, often overlooked some of the core tasks of maintaining and sustaining them beyond their early stages. Quite a few of the initiatives required teachers to develop new skills as mentors and tutors. Teachers were learning to 'run faster', but the toll in terms of overload and stress on some of them was, at times, rather obvious. Most 'change managers' had simply added, albeit unintentionally, to the burdens on colleagues; few had found ways of alleviating them.

In half the schools we studied there was a group of teachers whom we judged to be 'resistant'. The existence of such a group in a school was negatively correlated with many of our measures of change. A minority of the staff in these schools were weary and disconnected from the change processes which were going on around them. Earlier research has suggested that schools in trouble can sometimes become almost patho-logical cultures (Reynolds 1996; Stoll *et al.* 1996). In the present study, however, this did not appear to be the case. In only one of the schools was the 'resistance' particularly overt. However, the resisters' undoubted 'dissociation' contributed significantly to the somewhat patchy and unsystematic development efforts made in their schools.

We noted earlier that some schools had invested heavily in giving more responsibilities to pupils and that this approach was associated with more rapid improvement. While pupils were aware of shifts of emphasis, when we asked them directly about ways in which their schools had changed in recent years, their responses were mostly conditioned by changes to the physical appearance, facilities or learning environments. They seldom identified any general improvements in teaching and learn-ing, apart from greater provision of computers. However, they often mentioned the influence of particular teachers they considered effective and the importance of teachers' explanatory skills (cf. Rudduck *et al.* 1996). They had few other observations to make about *changes* which had occurred but did, in several cases, remark on their teachers' lack of consistency in implementing new initiatives along previously agreed lines.

Concern for teaching and learning

The importance of aspects of teaching and learning to changes in schools' effectiveness was not something we had fully anticipated before our fieldwork, although in retrospect perhaps it should have been. When members of the research team judged the extent of changes along various dimensions, other features of schools' development had seemed more prominent, especially those relating to school management. Such impressions had been confirmed by the teachers' assessments as well. Whereas, in some schools, as many as 80–90 per cent reported that there had been 'substantial' changes in their school's 'attitude and approach to planning' or the 'ways it was run and organized', in only two schools did around half or more of the staff report that there had been 'substantial' changes to the quality of teaching and learning.[1]

Part of the reason for these perceptions may have been that changes in teaching and learning were less obvious to individual members of staff than some of those which affected the whole school. If the SMT decides, for example, to change the way the school is run and organized this is likely to be very clear to all concerned. On the other hand, even if there have been changes to teaching and learning in a number of departments, knowledge of them may be largely confined to members of those departments. The changes may also have been slower, more incremental and consequently less evident. However, the main reason why this dimension of change emerged as important in our various analyses needs to be acknowledged – namely, its comparative prominence in rapidly improving schools and its almost total absence in slowly improving ones. In no case did more than a small proportion of the teachers in the slowly improving schools remark on substantial changes in the quality of teaching and learning.

It is difficult to generalize across schools about the nature of the changes they had initiated in relation to teaching and learning at classroom level beyond those imposed by changing National Curriculum requirements. Our general impression was that most had steered clear of additional curriculum innovations *per se*. Initiatives in teaching and learning had been rather limited and had occurred relatively late in the change programme. Many had focused on what might be termed 'traditional' supports for learning, such as monitoring homework arrangements, or immediate improvements to the learning environment and facilities (such as greater provision and use of IT and resources centres). They had also attempted to increase the amounts of 'learning time' available through timetable changes. Other areas where initiatives had been taken included: the reintroduction of textbooks to be kept and taken home by individual pupils; the increasing recognition that structured approaches to literacy might be useful (especially in Year 7); and the changing use of special educational needs staff to provide in-class support.

Sometimes departmental developments had begun to spill over into neighbouring departments. In one school, for example, the introduction of a textbook for science had prompted other departments to do something similar. In another, four departments had jointly planned the more systematic use of integrated learning systems. In a third, meanwhile, a decision had been made to revamp and co-ordinate homework policies across several departments.

In short, there was no single method (or group of methods) which the more successful schools had adopted. Given their rather different starting-points, it would probably be naive to expect one. If there was a common theme running across the schools which were improving more rapidly, it was that they had found ways of facilitating more discussion among colleagues about classroom issues than hitherto. Such changes were subtle but influential. There are echoes here of Rosenholtz's (1989) discussion of the differences between 'stuck' and 'moving' schools.

External influences on change

The schools in our study mostly felt that any improvements they had secured were largely of their own making, although such perceptions did not always seem justified.[2] They underestimated, in our view, the general impact of various national reforms. Moreover, where an Ofsted inspection had taken place either before or during the period of change with which we were concerned, there was some acknowledgement that it had acted as a spur for change and/or a further input to the change process. The introduction of league tables of schools' results had also contributed by 'pricking schools into action', as one head put it.

At the same time there were signs that LEA support had stimulated changes. The contributions of link advisers and the support of other LEA personnel with specific expertise to offer were spontaneously mentioned. LEA initiatives to provide schools with better data on their performance, such as value-added analyses and, a good deal more recently, breakdowns of performance by gender, had also proved influential.

Meanwhile SMTs had learnt to become more adept at promoting positive images for their schools. However, despite concerted efforts to improve, schools' 'reputations' in their local communities proved very resistant to change. Several of the schools felt that if they were to alter community perceptions they had to reach (or even exceed) the most optimistic expectations for their performance.

Routes to improvement?

The driving question behind our research has been about how schools improve. The schools in our study seem to have been engaged in three broad approaches which we characterize variously as tactics, strategies and capacity-building. While these do not map neatly on to the effectiveness and improvement trajectories of the different schools in our study, there was certainly some correspondence.

Nearly all the schools were operating at the level of *tactics*. They had focused (possibly for the first time and certainly more than previously) on outcome measures and identified some 'obvious' things they needed to do to improve their pupils' performance. Most had engaged, for example, in more monitoring of pupil performance, had entered at least some pupils for an extra exam and had focused rather more on providing support for 'borderline' candidates than in the past. In addition, they had probably reinforced some of these developments by revamping their codes of classroom conduct and homework policies at the same time. In the process they had begun to respond to the dictates of what more than one head called 'the improvement game'.

Responding simply at a tactical level presented problems for sustained improvement. Most of these initiatives proved to be demanding of staff energies, time and, to a lesser extent, resources. They involved sustaining teachers' commitment over lengthy periods. After two or three years their effects appear to have waned. Furthermore, as other schools picked up on the same agendas, the competitive edge attached to them began to diminish.[3] A narrowly tactical approach may be just enough to get a school that is lagging behind 'moving' but it is unlikely, without considerable ingenuity, to keep it going.

Our evidence suggests that the schools which were improving more 'rapidly' showed greater evidence of *strategic* thinking alongside their tactical approaches – see MacGilchrist *et al.* (1997) for further developments of this argument. They had almost invariably pulled the majority of the tactical levers but they were also more aware of their limitations. While attempting to develop whole-school policies, they focused more systematically on particular areas of weakness, encouraging and working with certain departments to help them get 'back on track'; sometimes they would set them specific 'targets'. At the same time they were reviewing the various approaches which might help to raise achievement levels across the institution. Their agendas had also begun to include some of the links between classroom practices and pupils' learning.

Schools which were developing along strategic lines undoubtedly did many of the things the purely tactical ones were engaged in. What marked them out, however, was the extent to which they were implementing co-ordinated responses to the challenges of school improvement. Of course, sustaining such commitments was also time-consuming and demanding; they did not always manage to do so. The departure of key staff members posed particular problems and challenges.

There has been a good deal of interest recently in the notion of continuous school improvement and whether at least some schools have succeeded in institutionalizing a 'capacity to improve'. Such thinking has stemmed in part from studies of 'learning organizations' in business (see, for example, Senge 1990) and gains further strength from the efforts of school developers to create something more permanent and self-sustaining (Fullan 1993; Leithwood and Louis 1998). But, as the research suggests, changing a school's core culture is likely to be a complex and long-term business (Hargreaves 1995). Indeed, while encouraging the teaching profession to sustain its commitment to long-term change, Fullan (1995) himself hints at the possibility that institutionalization of such a capacity is still a 'distant dream'.

While almost all the schools we studied in depth exhibited evidence of tactical approaches and several showed signs of strategic thinking, only two appeared to have moved beyond these stages. These two had a fairly sophisticated view of how to undertake change and 'pull all the relevant levers'. They were knowledgeable about the problems to be faced, believed that they had engaged with issues of teaching and learning for some time and were able to put forward fairly coherent rationales for the next steps.

What was interesting about both schools (and this marked them out from the others) was the extent to which they had shown a willingness to go beyond merely incremental approaches to change at some point in the not too distant past and engaged in some organizational restructuring with enhanced learning as an intended outcome. They had developed ways of being more specific about precisely how they wished to improve pupils' learning, were able to draw on colleagues' experiences to formulate strategies and had found ways of helping colleagues to evaluate and learn from their own and other teachers' classroom experiences. In their quest for higher performance they showed a willingness to engage with a wide range of potential sources of advice by encouraging their staffs to pursue their own professional development, providing in-house opportunities for development and support, seeking out help from their LEAs as well as finding ways of bringing in people from higher education and private consultants. In only one of the two schools, however, did the school's practices seem sufficiently well embedded for us to be confident in talking about its *capacity* to improve.[4] It would seem unwise to rely too heavily on approaches to change which assume that such a capacity is widely in place.

The importance of the 'learning level'

Our earlier analyses (see Chapter 10) indicated that schools which had developed 'policies for supporting teaching and learning' and which had begun to focus on ways of tackling 'the processes of teaching and learning' improved more rapidly. Correlations, of course, do not necessarily prove causation. However, these findings chime with an increasing interest in intervention at the 'learning level'.

Recent multi-level analyses have shown that there is considerable variation within schools at both departmental and classroom level (Bosker and Scheerens 1997; Creemers 1994). Partly as a result, there has been a refocusing on aspects of teacher effectiveness, a field which has been notably neglected over the last two decades.[5] Such developments have underlined the importance of changing teacher behaviours rather than merely hoping for school-level initiatives to ripple through to the classroom.

The development of greater awareness of 'learning level' strategies will probably be crucial to the next phase of school improvement. The departmental level in a school is closer to discussions about classroom practices in specific subjects and may, as a result, be more malleable. Even ineffective schools are likely to have some features which could serve as models of 'good practice'. In time, virtually every school could be expected to work on some aspect of its internal conditions from its own in-house resources. The prospects for transfer of good practice among people within the same buildings are likely to be better than transfer between schools. Teachers, in turn, will probably be more influenced by classroom-based policies that are closer to their main concerns with aspects of teaching and curriculum than by initiatives which they see as essentially top-down and managerial in origin and orientation. As our study shows, many heads of department, heads of year and subject co-ordinators were undoubtedly both willing and able to provide leadership within their schools. Schools' abilities to recognize their existing sources of leadership may need to be developed.

It must be acknowledged, however, that even in the 'leading-edge' schools there were considerable difficulties in directly addressing issues to do with teaching and learning; schools' efforts were mostly rather low-key. Their management teams had only recently begun to identify key teacher behaviours within the particular classrooms for which they were ultimately responsible and their 'insights' into classroom processes were often fairly rudimentary. Indeed, sometimes the ways in which these changes could be expected to impact directly upon pupils' achievements were unclear. To their credit the more rapidly improving schools were often aware that more had changed outside their classrooms than within them. However, systematic encouragement of teachers to engage in mutual observation and 'buddying' had only recently commenced. Emphasizing that 'teaching matters' had helped to create some momentum, but identifying the next steps was proving challenging.[6]

The constraints of context

Many of the teachers we talked to during the course of our research were convinced that the contexts within which their schools operated were at least as influential as any initiatives or strategies they might launch (Hopkins *et al.* in press). When teachers referred to their own schools' 'contexts' they were often commenting on the socio-economic characteristics of their catchment areas. By trying to take account of the intakes to the different schools in our study we attempted to cover some aspects of this concern. It may well be the case, however, that schools in particularly disadvantaged socio-economic contexts experience constraints which are *additional* to any shared with schools having comparably low-attaining intakes. There are glimpses in the North American literature of such 'context-specific' effects (Hallinger and Murphy 1986; Stringfield and Teddlie 1990). We also identified a number of other 'contextual' factors which struck us as potentially important. Our sample of case-study schools was, of course, too small to establish their effects in statistical terms.

The contrasting approaches of Rowland and Blackstone (both schools which improved rapidly) are relevant here. The improvement strategy at Blackstone was relatively straightforward. Its main ingredients were energy, optimism and a certain dynamism from the headteacher; structural changes to the school were modest. At first glance, the prognosis for such an unsophisticated approach might seem poor. In the event, and in the context of a depressed community which had suffered over the years, an 'up-front' approach to improvement proved to be quite potent. It is hard to imagine a similar 'strategy', however, being transferred to Rowland's more socially advantaged context or even starting to work there. The community's expectations of its school were very different.

A variety of other 'contextual' factors were thrown up during our fieldwork. Possibly the most important of these is what we termed the 'inheritance', the mix of personalities and attitudes which determine how close to the starting-gate a particular school is during any period of change. The age profile of the staff (too many nearing retirement and too few experienced recruits), the extent of staff turnover (either staying for very short periods or for ever), the leadership styles to which the staff have become accustomed (and in particular the kind of comfortable existence which top-down decision-making can sometimes create), and the presence of cliques resisting change (and reinforcing each other in their attitudes) all play a part in the equation.

At the same time a number of other factors which were external to the school also emerged. We did not, however, study any of these in great depth. They included the LEA's approach to supporting and improving its schools; whether the school had been in a position to take advantage of the additional resources made available through national initiatives (such as those allocated to schools going grant-maintained); and the extent of competition for pupils in the local market-place (an 'unpopular' school could find itself facing additional constraints as a result of reducing resources).

It is tempting to suggest that the problems facing schools in disadvantaged areas are somehow more formidable than those of schools serving more advantaged communities. On reflection, however, we began to realize that just as questions about schools' effectiveness need to take account of context, so too do those connected with improvement. A good deal of care is needed to ensure that schools are compared on a like-with-like basis regardless of whether one is looking at their effectiveness or their improvement. In practice, we suspect that we are not yet in a position to grasp what precisely the more important 'contextual' factors actually are. The research literature, which is the most likely place to find such discussions, is not yet oriented towards this kind of question. A school which has to cope with just one or two potentially constraining contextual factors may be able to make fairly rapid progress. Another, which seems outwardly similar but which has to deal with several simultaneously, may have to make at least a couple of attempts before it manages to take off.

Contemplating interventions beyond the immediate and familiar

The case studies in this book are all examples of what we would call 'naturally occurring' school improvement. While responding to nationally generated demands for change, schools were mostly devising their own solutions to them. As our study shows, however, many of them came up with the same answers notwithstanding their different starting-points.

Research studies certainly suggest that an element of 'reinventing the wheel' is necessary for successful implementation to occur. When one sees the same 'reinventions' occurring in school after school, however, one begins to wonder how literally this advice needs to be taken. More external support *was* probably available to the schools than they chose to take up; few of them, however, *consistently* sought assistance from 'outsiders' (their LEAs, higher education or other support agencies).

In short, schools perceived themselves to be part of a culture in which they were largely expected to seek out their own solutions. In such a situation, and operating with this kind of gestalt, there is a danger that all but the most confident will see requests for support as potential admissions of weakness.

As a result, many schools will be more comfortable with the view that 'their problems' are somehow unique to their situation. Armed with such an analysis they will begin to conclude that 'the solutions' are probably unique as well. Yet we know from our sample of schools (and a wide variety of other sources) that they perceive themselves to be facing a range of common and predictable educational challenges: boys' under-achievement; Year 7 pupils with literacy levels well below their chrono-logical reading ages; the dip in students' motivation and performance in Year 8; and so on.

The questions schools ask about innovations are, by now, very familiar. They are interested in:

- whether something 'works', which they increasingly tend to assess in terms of its effects on students' achievement;
- whether what is on offer is essentially a 'one size fits all' product or whether it offers several 'entry' levels and a sufficient range of posi-tions on what constitutes 'good practice';
- how demanding in terms of time and resources the innovation will be; and
- whether there are ways in which they can modify and adapt the pro-posed strategy to suit their own circumstances, with a view to 'owning' it.

Such questions are simple and direct enough. Unfortunately the answers schools get often seem to them to be equivocal. One of the reasons for this is, of course, that interventions in most educational settings are inherently complex and their impact *is* difficult to assess. Another, however, is that policy-makers, practitioners and researchers have been insufficiently active in evaluating the programmes they have been busily promoting.[7]

Given the amounts of time and energy schools are being asked to invest, we should have better answers by now. The reality is that we do not. But, as researchers remind us, 'learning partnerships' are not only at least a three-way process but also demand hard work on the part of all those involved (Rudduck and Wilcox 1988; Fullan 1993). The idea of sponsoring specific development programmes around key themes which explore and evaluate several possible routes towards similar ends needs to be taken a good deal more seriously in Britain than it has been to date.[8] Support networks of the kind which have been implemented in the USA and, to a lesser extent, in Britain would probably help schools to pursue their agendas more effectively.[9]

Meanwhile, some commentators have argued, while noting the kinds of reforms which schools have contemplated and attempted, that con-siderably bolder approaches are needed – for one of the fuller accounts of this position, see Barber (1996). The introduction of Education Action Zones, with their explicit commitment to a degree of experimentation, offers an important opportunity to explore some of these issues, albeit in contexts where many reforms have hitherto experienced difficulty in taking root.[10] The real challenge will be to ensure that such initiatives are rigorously evaluated.

Towards the third age of school improvement

We argued in an earlier chapter that research on school improvement had passed through at least two identifiable phases. It is clear that many of the key messages have been listened to in schools. Virtually every one of the 12 schools we studied in depth was attempting to improve itself. They had nearly all established some of the main change 'levers' and were busily pulling them. The problem that now needs to be faced is that too many of the changes schools were encouraged to explore had to do with aspects of their management, planning, organization and curriculum. As Michael Fullan (1993) has argued, it is the 'skills and habits of everyday teachers [which] are central to the future of learning societies'.

Research traditions serve a number of functions. One of them is to help shape the kinds of questions which need to be addressed. In the present study we have sought to merge the traditions of research on school effectiveness and school improvement. This has not proved easy and more work is needed. None the less, a few of the schools in our study offer some insights into the directions a 'third age' of research on school improvement will need to take. With the benefit of hindsight, it is now clear that insufficient attention was given in the earlier phases to ways of helping to influence what was going on in classrooms – the mix of teaching strategies, teacher behaviours and classroom conditions which determine what exactly it is that pupils learn. When schools and researchers finally succeed in unlocking these issues we shall be several steps closer to the goal of continuous improvement.

None of the schools in our study found sustaining a focus on teaching and learning straightforward. In an area where attitudes are so intimately bound up with notions of the professional self, many needed to be convinced that further change was necessary – their instinct was to resist. Others acknowledged the potential but remained doubtful about whether it could be released. Only for a minority was change definitely on the agenda. Their experiences point to some national priorities.

Modest amounts of external pressure had undoubtedly helped to make the case for improvement. In this of all areas, however, it was difficult to mandate or impose the conditions for change; prevailing perceptions of 'classroom realities' could not be ignored. The common challenge had been to find ways of linking insights generated through classroom observation and evaluation to a broader awareness of the opportunities for professional and institutional development. In some schools colleagues had observed each other at work; in others they had simply talked about it. The mix differed from school to school. But what the more 'rapidly improving' schools *had*, by one means or another, fumbled their ways towards was probably the most important resource of all – the unlocking of teachers' interests in changing their performance.

Notes

1 Indeed, high proportions of teachers in these particular schools claimed that there had been very few changes at all in this area.
2 Interestingly, in at least two of the three LEAs the advisory services subscribed to the view that it was 'important for schools to feel they were helping themselves'; this approach consequently informed a number of the ways in which the LEA interacted with schools requiring support.
3 The interest in 'shopping around' for the 'easiest' exam syllabuses, which was prevalent in several of our schools during the period covered by our research, is a case in point. Exam boards responded to the possibility by taking steps to ensure that the more obvious differences between them were minimized. And then, anticipating the advent of league tables, some schools began to enter their pupils for an extra exam subject. Between 1991 and 1993 the average number of exam subjects per pupil rose, as a result, from around 7.5 to 8.5. Non-examined subjects were one casualty as schools made space on their timetables to accommodate the change. The number of subjects entered then remained fairly constant in the following years. These kinds of changes tend to have short-term, largely one-off effects.
4 For a fuller account of some of the characteristics of schools as 'learning organizations', as well as a critique of some of the assumptions underlying such ideas, see Southworth (1994).
5 There has been increased interest in these issues over the last two or three years from a variety of different quarters. Awareness that there was substantial within-school variation probably associated with differences in teachers' effectiveness has been around, however, for the better part of two decades (Gray 1979).
6 Some possible frameworks for thinking about and developing these teaching-related issues are discussed in Joyce *et al.* (1997).
7 The area of boys' under-achievement is a case in point. Schools have identified (and been helped to identify) a major problem and have begun to seek solutions. Very few firm conclusions can, however, currently be offered (Arnot *et al.* 1998). Part of the reason for this is that, to date, most of the initiatives which policy-makers have sponsored have not been rigorously evaluated. Furthermore, some of the more promising ones have been very small-scale and have not been implemented on a sufficiently wide basis for worthwhile conclusions to be drawn.
8 In the USA, for example, Title One funding (for the educationally disadvantaged) has, over the years, been increasingly tied to the implementation of programmes which have a proven track record.
9 In the USA networks such as the Coalition of Essential Schools and the Accelerated Schools programme have become well established, although evidence on their 'success' is harder to come by. In Britain the scale of the initiatives is more modest. Examples include the Improving the Quality of Education for All programme, the High Reliability improvement project and a variety of teacher networks including ones focusing on such things as the interpretation of value-added approaches and teaching and learning.
10 What kinds of more systematic evidence emerge from this major programme will depend, of course, on how far its sponsors in the Standards and Effectiveness Unit at the DfEE succeed in persuading other policy-makers to adopt more rigorous approaches to evaluation.

REFERENCES

Aitkin, M. and Longford, N. (1986) Statistical modelling issues in school effectiveness studies, *Journal of the Royal Statistical Society*, Series A, 149(1): 1–43.

Arnot, M., Gray, J., James, M. and Rudduck, J. with Duveen, G. (1998) *Recent Research on Gender and Educational Performance*. London: Ofsted.

Ball, S.J. (1990) *Politics and Policy Making in Education*. London: Routledge.

Barber, M. (1996) *The Learning Game: Arguments for an Education Revolution*. London: Victor Gollancz.

Barber, M. and White, J. (eds) (1997) *Perspectives on School Improvement*. London University Institute of Education: Bedford Way Papers.

Berman, P. and McLaughlin, M. (1977) *Federal Programs Supporting Educational Change: Factors Affecting Implementation and Continuation*. Santa Monica, CA: Rand Corporation.

Bosker, R. and Scheerens, J. (1997) *The Foundations of Educational Effectiveness*. Oxford: Pergamon.

Brighouse, T. (1991) *What Makes a Good School?* Stafford: Network Educational Press.

Brookover, W.B., Beady, C., Flood, P., Schweitzer, J. and Wisenbaker, J. (1979) *Schools, Social Systems and Student Achievement: Schools Can Make a Difference*. New York: Praeger.

Brown, S., Riddell, S. and Duffield, J. (1996) Possibilities and problems of small-scale studies to unpack the findings of large-scale studies of school effectiveness, in J. Gray, D. Reynolds, C. Fitz-Gibbon and D. Jesson (eds), *Merging Traditions: The Future of Research on School Effectiveness and School Improvement*. London: Cassell.

Central Advisory Council for Education (1967) *Children and Their Primary Schools*, Volume I. London: HMSO.

Coleman, J.S., Campbell, E., Hobson, C., McPartland, J., Mood, A., Weinfeld, R. and York, R. (1966) *Equality of Educational Opportunity*. Washington, DC: US Government Printing Office.

Coleman, P. and Riley, K. (1995) Accentuate the positive, *Education*, 186: 11 and 18.

Comer, J. (1988) Educating poor minority children, *Scientific American*, November, 42–8.

Crandall, D. *et al.* (1982) *People, Policies and Practice: Examining the Chain of School Improvement*, Vols 1–10. Andover, MA: The Network.

Crandall, D., Eiseman, J. and Louis, K.S. (1986) Strategic planning issues that bear on the success of school improvement efforts, *Educational Administration Quarterly*, 22(2): 21–53.

Creemers, B. (1994) *The Effective Classroom*. London: Cassell.

Cuttance, P. (1994) Monitoring educational quality through performance indicators for school practice, *School Effectiveness and School Improvement*, 5(2): 101–26.

Daly, P. (1991) How large are school effects in Northern Ireland?, *School Effectiveness and School Improvement*, 2(4): 305–23.

Department for Education and Employment (1997a) *Excellence in Schools*. London: HMSO.

Department for Education and Employment (1997b) *From Targets to Action*. London: DfEE.

Department for Education and Employment and Ofsted (1995) *Governing Bodies and Effective Schools*. London: DfEE.

Department of Education and Science (1983) *School Standards and Spending: Statistical Analysis*. London: DES.

Department of Education and Science (1984) *School Standards and Spending: Statistical Analysis: A Further Appreciation*. London: DES.

Earley, P., Fidler, B. and Ouston, J. (eds) (1996) *Improvement through Inspection? Complementary Approaches to School Development*. London: David Fulton.

Edmonds, R.R. (1979) Effective schools for the urban poor, *Educational Leadership*, 37(10): 15–24.

Fitz-Gibbon, C.T. (1985) A-level results in comprehensive schools: The COMBSE project, year 1, *Oxford Review of Education*, 11(1): 43–58.

Fitz-Gibbon, C.T. (1991) Multilevel modelling in an indicator system, in S. Raudenbush and J.D. Willms, *Schools, Pupils and Classrooms: International Studies of Schooling from a Multilevel Perspective*. London and New York: Academic Press.

Fitz-Gibbon, C.T. (1992) School effects at 'A' level – genesis of an information system, in D. Reynolds and P. Cuttance (eds), *School Effectiveness: Research, Policy and Practice*. London: Cassell.

Fitz-Gibbon, C.T. (1996) *Monitoring Education*. London: Cassell.

Fitz-Gibbon, C.T. (1997) *The Value-Added National Project: Final Report*. London: School Curriculum and Assessment Authority.

Fitz-Gibbon, C.T., Tymms, P.B. and Hazlewood, R.D. (1989) Performance indicators and information systems, in D. Reynolds, B.P.M. Creemers, and T. Peters (eds), *School Effectiveness and Improvement: Selected Proceedings of the First International Congress for School Effectiveness*. Groningen, Netherlands: RION.

Freeman, J. and Teddlie, C. (1997) A phenomenological examination of 'naturally occurring' school improvement: Implications for democratisation of schools. Paper presented at the annual meeting of the American Educational Research Association, New York.

Fullan, M. (1982) *The Meaning of Educational Change*. New York: Teachers College Press.

Fullan, M. (1991) *The New Meaning of Educational Change*. London: Cassell.

Fullan, M. (1992) *Successful School Improvement*. Buckingham: Open University Press.

Fullan, M. (1993) *Change Forces: Probing the Depths of Educational Reform*. London: Falmer Press.

Fullan, M. (1995) The school as a learning organisation: distant dreams, *Theory into Practice*, 34(4): 230–5.

Fullan, M., Bennett, B. and Rolheiser-Bennett, C. (1990) Linking classroom and school improvement, *Educational Leadership*, 47(8): 13–19.

Glickman, C. (1990) Pushing school reforms to a new edge: the seven ironies of school empowerment, *Phi Delta Kappan*, 72(1): 68–75.

Goldstein, H. (1995) *Multilevel Models in Educational and Social Research*. A revised edition. London: Edward Arnold.

Goldstein, H. and Lewis, T. (eds) (1996) *Assessment: Problems, Developments and Statistical Issues*, Chichester: John Wiley.

Goldstein, H. and Spiegelhalter, D. (1996) League tables and their limitations: statistical issues in comparisons of institutional performance, *Journal of the Royal Statistical Society*, Series A, 159(3): 385–443.

Goldstein, H., Rasbash, J., Yang, M., Woodhouse, G., Pan, H., Nuttall, D. and Thomas, S. (1993) A multilevel analysis of school examination results, *Oxford Review of Education*, 19(4): 425–33.

Gray, J. (1979) Reading progress in English infant schools: some problems emerging from a study of teacher effectiveness, *British Educational Research Journal*, 5(2): 141–58.

Gray, J. (1981) A competitive edge: Examination results and the probable limits of secondary school effectiveness, *Educational Review*, 33(1): 25–35.

Gray, J. (1982) Towards effective schools: Problems and progress in British research, *British Educational Research Journal*, 7(1): 59–79.

Gray, J. (1997) A bit of a curate's egg? Three decades of official thinking about the quality of schools, *British Journal of Educational Studies*, 45(1): 4–21.

Gray, J. and Jesson, D. (1987) Exam results and local authority league tables, in A. Harrison and J. Gretton (eds), *Education and Training UK 1987*, Newbury: Policy Journals, pp. 33–41.

Gray, J. and Jesson, D. (1996) A nation on the move? The nature and extent of school improvement in the 1990s. Paper presented to the Annual Conference of the British Educational Research Association, Lancaster.

Gray, J. and Wilcox, B. (1995) *'Good School, Bad School': Evaluating Performance and Encouraging Improvement*. Buckingham: Open University Press.

Gray, J., McPherson, A.F. and Raffe, D. (1983) *Reconstructions of Secondary Education: Theory, Myth, and Practice since the War*. London: Routledge & Kegan Paul.

Gray, J., Jesson, D. and Jones, B. (1984) Predicting differences in examination results between local education authorities: Does school organisation matter?, *Oxford Review of Education*, 8(1).

Gray, J., Jesson, D. and Jones, B. (1986) The search for a fairer way of comparing schools' examination results, *Research Papers in Education*, 1(2): 91–122.

Gray, J., Jesson, D. and Sime, N. (1990) Estimating differences in the examination performance of secondary schools in six LEAs – a multilevel approach to school effectiveness, *Oxford Review of Education*, 16(2): 137–58.

Gray, J., Jesson, D., Goldstein, H., Hedger, K. and Rasbash, J. (1995) A multi-level analysis of school improvement: Changes in schools' performance over time, *School Effectiveness and School Improvement*, 6(2): 97–114.

Gray, J., Goldstein, H. and Jesson, D. (1996a) Changes and improvements in schools' effectiveness: trends over five years, *Research Papers in Education*, 11(1): 35–51.

Gray, J., Reynolds, D., Fitz-Gibbon, C. and Jesson, D. (eds) (1996b) *Merging Traditions: The Future of Research on School Effectiveness and School Improvement*. London: Cassell.

Hallinger, P. and Murphy, J. (1986) The social context of effective schools, *American Journal of Education*, 94: 328–55.

Hargreaves, A., and Reynolds, D. (eds) (1989) *Education Policy: Controversies and Critiques*. Lewes: Falmer Press.

Hargreaves, A., Liebermann, A., Fullan, M. and Hopkins, D. (eds) (1998) *International Handbook of Educational Change*, Dordrecht: Kluwer.

Hargreaves, D.H. (1995) School effectiveness, school change and school improvement: the relevance of the concept of culture, *School Effectiveness and School Improvement*, 6(1): 23–46.

Hargreaves, D.H. and Hopkins, D. (1991) *The Empowered School: The Management and Practice of Development Planning*. London: Cassell.

Harris, A., Jamieson, I. and Russ, J. (1995) A study of effective departments in secondary schools, *School Organisation*, 15(3): 283–99.

Hedger, K. and Jesson, D. (1998) *The Numbers Game: Using Assessment Data in Secondary Schools*. Shrewsbury: Shropshire LEA.

Hopkins, D. (ed.) (1987) *Improving the Quality of Schooling*. Lewes: Falmer Press.

Hopkins, D. (1990) The International School Improvement Project (ISIP) and effective schooling: Towards a synthesis, *School Organisation*, 10(3): 129–94.

Hopkins, D. and Harris, A. (1997) Understanding the school's capacity for development: growth states and strategies, *School Leadership and Management*, 17(3): 401–11.

Hopkins, D., Ainscow, M. and West, M. (1994) *School Improvement in an Era of Change*. London: Cassell.

Hopkins, D., West, M. and Ainscow, M. (1996) *Improving the Quality of Education for All*. London: David Fulton.

Hopkins, D., Reynolds, D. and Gray, J. (in press) Moving on and moving up: confronting the complexities of improvement, *Educational Research and Evaluation*.

Huberman, M. and Miles, M. (1984) *Innovation Up Close*. New York: Plenum.

Jencks, C., Smith, M., Acland, H., Bane, M., Cohen, D., Heyns, B. and Michelson, S. (1972) *Inequality: A Reassessment of the Effects of Family and Schooling in America*. London: Allen Lane.

Jesson, D. (1996) *Value-Added Measures of School GCSE Performance*. London: DfEE.

Jesson, D. and Gray, J. (1991) Slants on slopes: Using multi-level models to investigate differential school effectiveness and its impact on pupils' examination results, *School Effectiveness and School Improvement*, 2(3): 230–47.

Joyce, B. (1991) The doors to school improvement, *Educational Leadership*, 48(8): 59–62.

Joyce, B., Calhoun, E. and Hopkins, D. (1997) *Models for Learning – Tools for Teaching*. Buckingham: Open University Press.

Leithwood, K. and Louis, K.S. (1998) *Schools as Learning Organisations*. Lisse, Netherlands: Swets & Zeitlinger.

Louis, K. and Miles, M. (1991) Managing reform: Lessons from urban high schools, *School Effectiveness and School Improvement*, 2(2): 75–96.

Louis, K.S. and Miles, M. (1992) *Improving the Urban High School*. London: Cassell.
MacBeath, J., Boyd, B., Rand, J. and Bell, S. (1996) *Schools Speak for Themselves*. London: National Union of Teachers.
MacBeath, J. and Mortimore, P. (1994) Improving school effectiveness. Proposal for a research project for the Scottish Office Education Department, Glasgow, Quality in Education Centre, University of Strathclyde.
MacGilchrist, B., Myers, K. and Reed, J. (1997) *The Intelligent School*. London: Paul Chapman.
McLaughlin, M. (1990) The Rand change agent study revisited: Macro perspectives, micro realities. *Educational Researcher*, 19(9): 11–16.
Mortimore, P. (1996) *The Road to Success: Four Case Studies of Schools Which No Longer Require Special Measures*. London: DfEE.
Mortimore, P. (1998) *The Road to Improvement: Reflections on School Effectiveness*. Lisse, Netherlands: Swets & Zeitlinger.
Mortimore, P., Sammons, P., Stoll, L., Lewis, D. and Ecob, R. (1988) *School Matters: The Junior Years*. Wells: Open Books. (Reprinted in 1995 by Paul Chapman, London.)
Myers, K. (ed.) (1996) *School Improvement in Practice: The Schools Make a Difference Project*. London: Falmer Press.
National Commission on Education (1996) *Success against the Odds: Effective Schools in Disadvantaged Areas*. London: Routledge.
Newton, P. (1997) Examining standards over time, *Research Papers in Education*, 12(3): 227–48.
Nisbet, J. (ed.) (1973) *Creativity of the School*. Paris: OECD.
Nuttall, D.L., Goldstein, M., Prosser, R. and Rasbash, J. (1989) Differential school effectiveness, *International Journal of Educational Research*, 13(7): 769–76.
Ofsted (1994) *Improving Schools*. London: HMSO.
Ofsted (1995) *The Annual Report of Her Majesty's Chief Inspector of Schools*. London: HMSO.
Ofsted (1996) *The Annual Report of Her Majesty's Chief Inspector of Schools 1994/95*. London: HMSO.
Ofsted (1997a) *From Failure to Success: How Special Measures Are Helping Schools Improve*. London: Ofsted.
Ofsted (1997b) *LEA Support for School Improvement: A Framework for the Inspection of Local Education Authorities*. London: Ofsted.
Reynolds, D. (1988) British school improvement research: the contribution of qualitative studies, *International Journal of Qualitative Studies in Education*, 1(2): 143–54.
Reynolds, D. (1991) Changing ineffective schools, in M. Ainscow (ed.), *Effective Schools for All*. London: David Fulton.
Reynolds, D. (1996) Turning round ineffective schools, in J. Gray, D. Reynolds, C. Fitz-Gibbon and D. Jesson (eds), *Merging Traditions: The Future of Research on School Effectiveness and School Improvement*. London: Cassell.
Reynolds, D. and Cuttance, P. (eds) (1992) *School Effectiveness: Research, Policy and Practice*. London: Cassell.
Reynolds, D. and Farrell, S. (1996) *Worlds Apart? – A Review of International Studies of Educational Achievement Involving England*. London: HMSO for Ofsted.
Reynolds, D., Sullivan, M. and Murgatroyd, S.J. (1987) *The Comprehensive Experiment*. Lewes: Falmer Press.

Reynolds, D., Hopkins, D. and Stoll, L. (1993) Linking school effectiveness knowledge and school improvement practice: towards a synergy, *School Effectiveness and School Improvement*, 4(1): 37–58.

Reynolds, D., Creemers, B., Nesselrodt, P., Schaffer, E., Stringfield, S. and Teddlie, C. (1994) *Advances in School Effectiveness Research and Practice*. Oxford: Pergamon.

Reynolds, D., Bollen, R., Creemers, B., Hopkins, D., Stoll, L. and Lagerweij, N. (eds) (1996) *Making Good Schools: Linking School Effectiveness and School Improvement*. London: Routledge.

Riley, K. and Rowles, D. (1997) *From Intensive Care to Recovery: Schools Requiring Special Measures*. London: Haringey LEA.

Rosenholtz, S. (1989) *Teachers' Workplace: The Social Organisation of Schools*. New York: Longman.

Rudduck, J. and Wilcox, B. (1988) Issues of ownership and partnership in school-centred innovation, *Research Papers in Education*, 3(3): 157–69.

Rudduck, J., Chaplain, R. and Wallace, G. (1996) *School Improvement: What Can Pupils Tell Us?* London: David Fulton.

Rutter, M., Maughan, B., Mortimore, P. and Ouston, J. with Smith, A. (1979) *Fifteen Thousand Hours: Secondary Schools and Their Effects on Children*. London: Open Books; and Boston: Harvard University Press.

Sammons, P., Nuttall, D. and Cuttance, P. (1993) Differential school effectiveness: Results from a re-analysis of the Inner London Education Authority's junior school project data, *British Educational Research Journal*, 19(4): 381–405.

Sammons, P., Hillman, J. and Mortimore, P. (1994) *Key Characteristics of Effective Schools: A Review of School Effectiveness Research*. London: Ofsted.

Sammons, P., Nuttall, D., Cuttance, P. and Thomas, S. (1995) Continuity of school effects: A longitudinal analysis of primary and secondary school effects on GCSE performance, *School Effectiveness and School Improvement*, 6(4): 285–307.

Sammons, P., Thomas, S. and Mortimore, P. (1997) *Forging Links: Effective Schools and Effective Departments*. London: Paul Chapman.

Scheerens, J. (1992) *Effective Schooling: Research, Theory and Practice*. London: Cassell.

Sebba, J., Gray, J. and West, M. (1998) *Sharpening the Focus: SE GEST, Improvement and Raising Standards*. London: DfEE.

Senge, P. (1990) *The Fifth Discipline: The Art and Practice of the Learning Organisation*. London: Century Business.

Silver, H. (1994) *Good Schools, Effective Schools*. London: Cassell.

Sizer, T. (1989) Diverse practice, shared ideas: The essential school, in H. Walberg and J. Lane (eds), *Organising for Learning: Towards the 21st Century*. Reston, VA: NASSP.

Slavin, R. (1995) Sands, bricks and seeds: School change strategies and readiness for reform. Paper presented to the Office of Educational Research and Improvement, US Department of Education.

Slavin, R.E. (1996) *Education for All*. Lisse, Netherlands: Swets & Zeitlinger.

Slee, R., Weiner, G. and Tomlinson, S. (eds) (1998) *School Effectiveness for Whom? Challenges to the School Effectiveness and School Improvement Movements*. London: Falmer Press.

Smith, D.J. and Tomlinson, S. (1989) *The School Effect. A Study of Multi-racial Comprehensives*. London: Policy Studies Institute.

Southworth, G. (1994) The learning school, in P. Ribbins and E. Burridge (eds), *Improving Education: Promoting Quality in Schools*. London: Cassell, pp. 52–72.

Southworth, G. and Sebba, J. (1997) Increasing the LEA's capacity to support schools as they seek to improve. Paper presented to annual conference of British Educational Research Association, York.

Steedman, J. (1980) *Progress in Secondary Schools*. London: National Children's Bureau.

Steedman, J. (1983) *Examination Results in Selective and Non-selective Schools*. London: National Children's Bureau.

Stoll, L. and Fink, D. (1994) School effectiveness and school improvement: voices from the field, *School Effectiveness and School Improvement*, 5(2): 149–77.

Stoll, L. and Fink, D. (1996) *Changing Our Schools: Linking School Effectiveness and School Improvement*. Buckingham: Open University Press.

Stoll, L. and Myers, K. (eds) (1997) *No Quick Fixes: Perspectives on Schools in Difficulty*. London: Falmer Press.

Stoll, L. and Thomson, M. (1996) Moving together: a partnership approach to improvement, in P. Earley, B. Fidler and J. Ouston (eds), *Improvement through Inspection?* London: David Fulton.

Stoll, L., Myers, K. and Reynolds, D. (1996) Understanding ineffectiveness. Paper presented at the annual meeting of the American Educational Research Association, New York.

Stringfield, S. and Reynolds, D. (1996) Failure free schooling is ready for take off. *Times Educational Supplement*, 19 January, Supplement, p. 10.

Stringfield, S. and Teddlie, C. (1990) School improvement efforts: qualitative and quantitative data from four naturally occurring experiments in Phases 3 and 4 of the Louisiana School Effectiveness Study, *School Effectiveness and School Improvement*, 1(2): 139–61.

Stringfield, S., Winfield, L., Millsap, M.A., Puma, M.J., Gamse, B. and Randall, B. (1994) *Urban and Suburban/Rural Special Strategies*. Washington, DC: US Department of Education.

Stringfield, S., Millsap, M.A. and Herman, R. (1997) *Urban and Suburban/Rural Special Strategies for Educating Disadvantaged Children: Findings and Policy Implications of a Longitudinal Study*. Washington, DC: US Department of Education.

Teddlie, C. and Stringfield, S. (1993) *Schools Do Make a Difference: Lessons Learned from a Ten-year Study of School Effects*. New York: Teachers College Press.

Thomas, S. and Mortimore, P. (1996) Comparison of value-added models for secondary school effectiveness, *Research Papers in Education*, 11(1): 5–33.

Thomas, S., Sammons, P. and Mortimore, P. (1995) Determining what adds value to student achievement, *Educational Leadership International*, 58(6): 19–22.

Tymms, P.B. (1997) *The Value-Added National Project: Technical Reports Primary 3 and Primary 4*. London: School Curriculum and Assessment Authority.

van Velzen, W., Miles, M., Ekholm, M., Hameyer, U. and Robin, D. (1985) *Making School Improvement Work: A Conceptual Guide to Practice*. Leuven, Belgium: ACCO.

Whatford, C. (1997) Rising from the ashes, in L. Stoll and K. Myers (eds), *No Quick Fixes*. London: Falmer Press.

Wilcox, B. (1997) Schooling, school improvement and the relevance of Alasdair MacIntyre, *Cambridge Journal of Education*, 27(2): 249–60.

Wilcox, B. and Gray, J. (1996) *Inspecting Schools: Holding Schools to Account and Helping Schools to Improve*. Buckingham: Open University Press.

Wilcox, B., Wilcox, J. and Gray, J. (1996) Getting into the pack: School improvement in context. Paper presented to the Annual Conference of the British Educational Research Association, Lancaster.

Willms, J.D. (1985) The balance thesis – contextual effects of ability on pupils' 'O' grade examination results, *Oxford Review of Education*, 11(1): 33–41.

Willms, J.D. (1986) Social class segregation and its relationship to pupils' examination results in Scotland, *American Sociological Review*, 51(2): 224–41.

Willms, J.D. (1987) Differences between Scottish educational authorities in their educational attainment, *Oxford Review of Education*, 13(2): 211–32.

Willms, J.D. and Cuttance, P. (1985) School effects in Scottish secondary schools, *British Journal of Sociology of Education*, 6(3): 289–305.

Woodhouse, G. and Goldstein, H. (1988) Educational performance indicators and LEA league tables. *Oxford Review of Education*, 14(3): 301–20.

NAME INDEX

SUBJECT INDEX